LAUNCHING A LEADERSHIP REVOLUTION

MASTERING THE FIVE LEVELS OF INFLUENCE

CHRIS BRADY | ORRIN WOODWARD

OBSTACLES
PRESS

First Edition, November 2013
10 9 8 7 6 5 4 3 2

Published by:

Obstaclés Press
4072 Market Place Dr.
Flint, MI 48507

Unless otherwise noted, all Scripture quotations are taken from *The Holy Bible, King James Version*, Cambridge, 1769.

Scripture quotations marked "NKJV" are taken from *The New King James Version*/ Thomas Nelson Publishers, Nashville : Thomas Nelson Publishers., Copyright © 1982. Used by permission. All rights reserved.

Scripture quotations marked "NASB" are taken from the *New American Standard Bible*, Copyright © 1960, 1962, 1963, 1971, 1972, 1973, 1975, 1977, 1995 by The Lockman Foundation. Used by permission.

www.life-leadership-home.com
www.life-leadership-home.ca

ISBN 978-0-9895763-6-9

Layout by Norm Williams, nwa-inc.com

Printed in the United States of America

CONTENTS

PREFACE

We were in the beautiful British Virgin Islands with our wives one evening when we were struck with the inspiration for what would eventually become the book *Launching a Leadership Revolution*. It was late at night, stars beamed brightly overhead, a warm tropical breeze wafted across the veranda, and we couldn't sleep. We'd gotten into a discussion about the essence of leadership. It began with a simple enough question: "Given equal starting points and conditions, why do some people succeed, while others don't?" And it developed into a full-fledged investigation. Our wives lost interest and headed to bed, while the two of us continued to hash out our theories deep into the night.

At one point, we began writing down words in an attempt to capture the concept of leadership—*courage, integrity, vision, execution, influence, impact*—until eventually we had nothing more than hollow-sounding platitudes that grew increasingly meaningless as we added to the stack. We erased what we'd written and began again. This time we changed the question: "What is the difference between those who succeed and those who don't?" The change in the question was subtle, but as always seems to happen when one properly defines a problem, the answer was immediately available. "Hunger," we said in near unison. Hunger.

Looking back, we now realize it was a radical idea. To think that internal desire could be the one unifying factor in the concept of leadership almost seems too simple, but again and again, as we dug further into our research, we found it to be true. All great leaders, big and small, have in common an internal hunger to make a difference, contribution, change, or improvement. It's really that simple.

Therefore, as we wrote the book, the entire construct was built upon the idea that anyone and everyone can lead, but they would all require the internal ingredient of hunger to do so. There were no ideal personalities or positions, and there were no stereotypical models of those "born" into leadership. Instead, what we found were people of every stripe who had achieved influence and impact in the lives of others through leadership that grew out of an internal desire. Period.

As our book got out into the marketplace and gained traction, eventually hitting the top of the *New York Times* business bestseller list, what we heard from readers again and again was that they had never realized the key role hunger played in the positive influence of others. It seemed our realization was resonating with readers as much as it had with us. And for anyone seeking to use his or her talents and gifts to make a difference in the world, there couldn't be better news. Ultimately, the ramifications of our assertion meant that anyone anywhere could be a leader, in big ways and small, in any category or application. All that was needed was the hunger to do so, and that could and would lead to everything else required.

Another development occurred as the book took flight, making its way into six additional languages and being used by colleges and consultants alike: there was a growing demand for a workbook companion. Readers were hungry for more and wanted to dig deeper into practical applications and interaction. The workbook you hold in your hands is the result of nearly eight years of such marketplace demand. It was never envisioned or foreseen in any way by the authors, who were busy building businesses, launching new companies, and generally living the things about which we had written. We are businessmen and leaders first, authors second, a fact that has become a point of contention with some of our kinder readers (whose patience is greatly appreciated). Still, we feel reassured that this may in fact contribute inestimable value to what we do write—it is the product of experience and not theory. It is our hope that this excuse for our tardiness in producing this volume will be sufficient.

This interactive companion to *Launching a Leadership Revolution* is designed to increase the understanding of the information presented in the original book. Through an interactive learning process, it is our intent that the readers (or should we say *participants*) not only gain a better knowledge of the material, but also make better use of it. This can only happen as useful information leaves the realm of theory and enters into that of application. That is the purpose of this publication.

Many of the stories and illustrations will seem familiar, but their reinclusion here is by design, repetition being the mother of mastery. However, we have brought much new material to these pages too, in the hope of increasing reader interest and also because we just couldn't help it. Eight years of experience since the original publication has taught us much, and we can't resist "piling on." We hope you deem this to be to your advantage.

Finally, we wish to congratulate you for digging into this volume. The very act of doing so indicates a lot about your journey as a leader. After all, the hunger to learn is the first step, and you're already there. Proceed with passion!

INTRODUCTION

We began *Launching a Leadership Revolution* with a story about a man named Ira Yates and use that as our starting point here as well.

Just before the Great Depression, a man named Ira Yates sold his profitable business to return to the ranching life he had known growing up. He bought a thousand acres in west Texas and struggled through the years of the Depression, barely able to make a living. As he heard rumors of Texas oil fields being discovered, he decided to drill on his ranch, but had difficulty getting oil companies to assist him with the complicated process. Finally, Yates set up a test rig and found that he was living above one of the largest oil fields in North America. His fortune was made.

Leadership ability is a lot like the drilling equipment used by Yates and his partners to discover the richness of oil that already existed beneath him. Each of us has a natural wellspring of talent and ability buried within. The drill of leadership is required to tap into the geyser of our potential. As with Yates's drilling equipment, leadership ability will take effort to attain, but the rewards are incalculable.

Do you believe leadership ability is latent in everyone and all that is needed is to tap into it? Explain.

_____

_____

_____

Who do you know who has grown in his or her leadership ability beyond what may have previously been conceivable?

_____

_____

_____

Specifically how has that person grown?

_____

_____

_____

Are you convinced that leadership is like the drilling equipment Yates used to tap into his oil—in other words, that leadership is a tool that brings out hidden individual worth?

_____

_____

_____

One of our big beliefs is that leadership is for everyone. How does this break the traditional leadership paradigm?

_____

_____

_____

Do you feel you possess more capability than you are currently utilizing?

_____

_____

_____

Everyone is called upon to lead at some point in his or her life. Sometimes this occurs in big, visible ways, while at other times, it is only in small situations. It may be in a corporate setting, in small business ownership, in the educational process, from a position of authority or from a position of subordination, in the home or in the church, in the financial markets or in depressed countries, in the public eye or in private, but make no mistake: leadership will be required of everyone and at many times over the course of each person's life. The biggest question is will the person called to lead be ready?

Do you believe that sooner or later everyone will be called upon to lead?

_____

_____

_____

List three occasions in which you were expected or required to take leadership.

1. _____
2. _____
3. _____

On a scale of 1 to 5, with 1 being "terrible" and 5 being "excellent," rate your leadership performance in each of the situations you listed. Then for each, tell why you gave yourself that rating.

_____

_____

_____

In looking at these three situations, what is the biggest thing you've learned about your leadership ability?

_____

_____

_____

What did you do right in those situations?

_____

_____

_____

Author Noel Tichy wrote, "In a broad sense, what leaders do is stage revolutions." The term _revolution_ is defined by Webster as "an activity or movement designed to effect fundamental changes." In the beginning, revolutions start with the unrest of one person or perhaps a small group of individuals. These early leaders begin working to influence people and events in a direction that assaults the status quo. Things can no longer remain as they were. Changes must be made. Usually because of their passion for the ideals espoused by the leaders, others are drawn into the effort. Gradually, talent and support are attracted from a broader and broader reach. As a tiny campfire grows into a large bonfire with increased fuel and oxygen supply, so too does a revolution grow in power and potency as fundamental changes are made and the results of those changes start to surface.

Sometimes a bonfire ends up engulfing the woods around it as it grows into a forest fire. It can never be forgotten, though, that all big fires start with a tiny spark. Similarly, all revolutions start as small rebellions. Fundamental changes are wrought because somewhere, somehow, someone decided to lead. One person can make a difference. One person leading *does* make a difference.

Name an instance with which you are familiar (either from history or from personal experience) when a revolution of change was brought about as described above.

_____

_____

_____

Who were the individuals involved at the beginning?

_____

_____

_____

What was the status quo that was being attacked?

_____

_____

_____

How did the idea spread and grow into a roaring fire?

_____

_____

_____

What did those early individuals do to lead that change?

_____

_____

_____

Do you agree that such revolutionary change always begins with a little spark?

_____

_____

_____

Looking deeper at this concept, don't miss the fact that *change* is always part of leadership. In other words, leadership really isn't about maintaining things as they are. It's about making things different. In fact, wherever there is a leader, the status quo is in danger of being forcefully overthrown.

So what is always part of leadership?

_____

_____

_____

And leadership will always attack what?

_____

_____

_____

So if the aim of leadership is change, it follows then that the aim of management is maintenance. Both are necessary to the survival of any organization, club, cause, or community, but they are different. Leadership is about doing the right things; management is about doing those things in the right way. Both are vital, but each has its place.

Leadership is about doing _____ _____

_____.

Management is about doing those things _____

_____ _____ _____.

Life should be about purpose and meaning and cause and fulfilling our personal, God-given destinies. Without exception, this is achieved through, with, and for *people*. In other words, it's done through leadership. Ken Kesey writes, "You don't lead by pointing a finger and telling people some place to go. You lead by going to that place and making a case." It is our intention that the exercises and material in this workbook will go to a certain place and make a compelling case. The *place* is the wellspring of your personal potential and that of your organization. The *case* we wish to make is that your potential is bountiful and sufficient to fulfill your life's calling. It sits there now, waiting to be tapped. This is accomplished by taking responsibility to lead in the areas of your life where you have been called. As you grow in your leadership ability, you will revolutionize your life.

Leadership is with, through, and for _____.

WHAT A LEADER IS

CHAPTER 1

Leadership Discussion

Sometimes if you want to see a change for the better, you have to take things into your own hands.

—CLINT EASTWOOD

A Question of Leadership

We find ourselves in a time when leadership is sorely needed. From the chaos, confusion, and rampant mediocrity that we find in our schools, churches, workplaces, families, personal lives, national politics, and international relations, the same questions seem to echo: "Will somebody please lead?" "Isn't there anybody who can fix this?" "Is there anyone who can make sense of all this?" "Is there anyone who cares enough to take responsibility for improvement here?" "Where are the leaders?" "Do heroes even exist anymore?"

These questions and more flow freely. Everybody seems to have an innate sense that something is needed. It is not hard to identify problems in a given situation. Making suggestions for changes and modifications is not difficult, either. Coming up with good ideas is no big deal. The world is full of great ideas and deep thinkers of grand theories. Implementation and results make the difference. They separate the heroes from the rest. And implementation with results, in any field or endeavor, takes leadership.

What Is Leadership?

The concept of "leadership" is a complex one. Most everybody has a feel for what the term means, at least in a general sense, but generalizations about leadership don't help us very much. In order to understand how to lead and why to lead and what it even means to lead, we'd better get clear on what comprises this complex idea embodied in this simple little English word.

What is your definition of leadership? Write some words and phrases that describe your current understanding of leadership.

_____

_____

_____

At this point, it may be helpful to turn to some experts. Surely they can shed some light on this subject. The list that follows is just a short offering:

- James C. Hunter: "We define leadership…as a skill of influencing people to work enthusiastically toward goals identified as being for the common good."
- Al Kaltman: "The successful leader gets superior performance from ordinary people."
- Bill George: "The leader's job is to provide an empowering environment that enables employees to serve their customers

and provides them the training, education, and support they need."

- Andy Stanley: "Leaders provide a mental picture of a preferred future and then ask people to follow them there."
- Vance Packard: "Leadership is getting others to want to do something that you are convinced should be done."
- Garry Wills: "Leadership is mobilizing others toward a goal shared by the leader and followers."
- Alan Keith: "Leadership is ultimately about creating a way for people to contribute to making something extraordinary happen."
- George Barna: "Leadership is the process of motivating, mobilizing, resourcing, and directing people to passionately and strategically pursue a vision from God that a group jointly embraces."
- Dwight D. Eisenhower: "Leadership is the art of getting someone else to do something you want done because he wants to do it."

Has your understanding/definition of leadership changed?

_____

_____

What were some of the key words or phrases that gave you a better understanding of what leadership is?

_____

_____

_____

These insights and definitions are good and helpful, and some we like particularly. But John Maxwell gives an exemplary definition, quoted here at length from his book *The 21 Irrefutable Laws of Leadership*:

> Leadership is influence—nothing more, nothing less. People have so many misconceptions about leadership. When they hear that someone has an impressive title or an assigned leadership position, they assume that he is a leader. Sometimes that's true. But titles don't have much value when it comes to leading. True leadership cannot be awarded, appointed, or assigned. It comes only from influence, and that can't be mandated. It must be earned.

What, then, is *influence*? Our favorite explanation of influence comes to us from nineteenth-century preacher and author Albert Barnes: "Influence is that in a man's known talents, learning, character, experience, and position, on which a presumption is based that what he holds is true; that what he proposes is wise."

George Barna tells us, "To be effective, a leader must have influence. But influence is a *product* of great leadership; it is not synonymous with it. You can have influence in a person's life without leading him anywhere."

In one word, what is the simplest way to determine if someone is a leader? _____

If "leadership is influence," who are the main leaders in your industry? What influence do they have over industry trends and standards?

_____

_____

_____

Within your organization, do you know anyone who is not formally recognized as a leader but has influence with others?

_____

List at least three ways you could increase your influence in your organization.

1. _____
2. _____
3. _____

Perhaps there will never be a short, cute definition for leadership. We are certain there will never be one upon which all "experts" agree. This difficulty in arriving at a concise explanation for the concept illustrates the enormity of the subject at hand. But all of the above definitions hit near the same mark. Any attempts to be more concise or specific are like trying to grab smoke. For the purpose of this study, then, we will fuse the above commentary into the following:

Leadership is the influence of others in a productive, vision-driven direction and is facilitated through the example, conviction, and character of the leader.

Do you agree with our definition of *leadership*? Explain.

_____

_____

_____

Whom do you know personally or from history who had influence with others but not in a productive way? Explain.

_____

_____

_____

Whom do you know personally or from history who had influence with others but not in a vision-driven direction? Explain.

_____

_____

_____

Leaders need to create a positive, productive leadership culture. Give an example of a positive leadership culture you have experienced.

_____

_____

_____

Give an example of a culture that was the opposite.

_____

_____

_____

What were the effects of each on the people and the productivity? How would you explain the experiences overall?

_____

_____

_____

Would you consider yourself to be a leader? Whom do you influence?

_____

_____

_____

Why Leadership?

We have surveyed the thoughts of many great minds on the definition of leadership, and as with a complex painting, the image is getting clearer the more we work with it. To brush in more detail, we must discuss the *purpose* of leadership.

Many people are interested in leadership for what they imagine it can provide them, including:

- Power
- Control
- Perks or being served

List an experience where you observed someone with the above expectations of leadership. What was the person's long-term result with these goals? How effective was his or her influence with others?

_____

_____

_____

But the life of a leader is quite different from such expectations. The life of a leader involves:

- Giving power (empowering)
- Helping others fix problems and move forward
- Serving others

List an experience where you observed someone with the above expectations of leadership. What was that person's long-term result with these goals? How effective was his or her influence with others?

In what ways can you discern someone's expectations of leadership?

Leaders lead for the joy of creating something bigger than themselves. Noted leadership consultant Warren Bennis says that he wants to publish books "that disturb the present in the service of a better future." That's good, and it's a sentiment shared by Hyrum Smith: "Leaders conduct planned conflict against the status quo."

To illustrate, consider the story of Ray Kroc and the making of the McDonald's fast-food empire. Kroc discovered the little McDonald's restaurant in Southern California in the 1950s and was amazed. The McDonald brothers had developed an efficient, unique, and highly profitable operation. They had fast-food production and delivery down to a science, and they were making what they considered a lot of money. But Kroc saw further. He realized that their little restaurant could be copied and duplicated and reproduced around the nation, and he set about trying to make that happen. Author Jim Collins, in *Good to Great*, explained that great leaders have ambition beyond their own personal self-interest. They are not satisfied with personal success only, but focus almost entirely upon furthering the vision of the *enterprise*.

At first Kroc attempted partnering with the McDonald brothers, but he found this restrictive and an anchor on his progress. Then he tried buying rights to their system for a period of ten years. But again, his vision outran theirs, and he found the provisions contained within the contract to be incompatible with his vision. The McDonald brothers were content. Kroc was not.

So if leadership is influence applied toward an overarching vision (pun intended), it follows that this influence is motivated by discontent with the status quo and directed toward something better. We like to call this "making a difference." And leaders do that in the direction of their vision for the future, a vision that sees further than others see. That is what it means to *lead*.

Leaders lead for the joy of creating something _____ _____ _____.

Leaders conduct planned conflict against _____ _____ _____.

The McDonald brothers had a very successful operation. Why did Ray Kroc want to change what they were doing?

_____

_____

_____

Results

The level of leadership determines the success of its results. Over time, where there are lackluster results, there is a leadership deficiency. Where there are stellar results, there is strong leadership. John Maxwell says that "everything rises and falls on leadership."

The War of 1812 was a perilous time for the brand-new United States. Only a few decades old, the young country found itself embroiled in yet another war with England. With the exception of a very impressive string of naval victories, the United States had been battered at the hands of the British. Washington, the national capital that was still under construction, had been not only successfully invaded but also humiliatingly burned. While a treaty of sorts had been signed between the two nations, the British knew that word of the peace would not travel fast enough to stop the invading force they'd sent to attack the city of New Orleans.

New Orleans was a strategically pivotal city. Most of the trade from the North American west flowed down the Mississippi and through New Orleans at the base of the river's delta. If New Orleans were lost, Britain believed it could split the United States in half and force a treaty more favorable to its side. With the positive conclusion of an invasion of New Orleans, there would be time for the British parliament to reject the current terms and negotiate a much stiffer peace.

The confidence of the New Orleans leadership to fend off an attack was receding like an ebb tide. The Committee for the Safety of New Orleans issued a report itemizing the poor morale and lack of preparations by the local militia in defense of the city. The city had transferred from the hands of the Spanish to the French and finally to the United States in less than a decade, and the loyalty of her defenders was a major concern. In fact, the speaker of the Louisiana senate considered surrendering the city to the British without a fight because most inhabitants were more loyal to the city than to the United States. Additionally, there was the very real fear of a slave rebellion in the area.

By contrast, the British were confident. Riding high on their recent gains in the Napoleonic Wars, they expected a decisive rout at New Orleans. They were battle tested and proven, and certainly no ragtag multicultural militia could match their might.

In the case of the defense of New Orleans in the War of 1812, the tragedy of poor leadership is quite clear. The results are similar to the results of bad leadership elsewhere, whether in industry, in politics, or in the home, though they may not be fatal. Chaos, lack of progress, confusion, and frustration are sure to follow where leaders refuse or fail to lead.

Now let's observe *real leadership* in action by resuming our look at the Battle of New Orleans.

Into this storm marched Major General Andrew Jackson. Only Andrew Jackson's indomitable will and courageous leadership stood between an acceptable peace treaty and the potential destruction of the United States. With only his small Tennessee militia, Jackson arrived on the scene just in time to bring order out of chaos and resolve out of fear. Assuming leadership of a patchwork army made up of the Louisiana militia, a band of local pirates, and several hundred black volunteers from Haiti, Jackson headed a force that amounted to just over half the total available to the British invaders.

Quick and creative defense works allowed Jackson's badly outnumbered and outclassed army to perform at a level way above its strength. The battle opened with an intense artillery barrage, but Jackson's personal courage steeled the resolve of his men to endure in the face of overwhelming odds. Intense combat followed as the heroes of Europe slammed their best troops against Jackson's forces. Jackson shrewdly deployed his troops to meet every British challenge, much of the early fighting turning into hand-to-hand slugfests. Unable to advance and suffering heavy losses, the British lines eventually gave way. The battle turned into a rout of the British. Three top British generals were killed in what became the most lopsided battle of the war. Within a few hundred yards lay nearly one thousand dead and dying British. The American side suffered thirteen killed and wounded.

The Battle of New Orleans, as it came to be called, allowed the treaty ending the conflict to be ratified and the War of 1812 to end.

The difference between the early pessimism of the New Orleans defenders and the final American result was due directly to the leadership and decision making of General Andrew Jackson.

It was the same company, the same men, the same battle, the same enemy, but a different leader that dramatically turned the tide. The strength of the leadership makes all the difference.

Everything rises and falls on _____.

How noticeable is the difference between poor and great leadership in an organization?

_____

_____

_____

How important was it for New Orleans to have strong leadership during this time?

_____

_____

_____

What do you think might have happened if New Orleans had had poor leadership during the battle?

_____

_____

_____

Things looked bleak for New Orleans before the battle with the British. But when the battle was over, the Americans had won an enormous victory. What was the difference between before and after?

_____

_____

_____

Think about the different bosses (or coaches, ministry leaders, teachers, etc.) you've had in the past. How would you describe the worst one? How about the best one? What were the greatest differences?

_____

_____

_____

Cultivating Leadership

Circle True or False.

True/False   Not everyone has what it takes to be a leader.

True/False   Only certain personalities can become leaders.

So how does one acquire leadership? The very asking of that question presupposes a very important first point: _Leadership ability can be acquired_. Some say leaders are born, that they come into the world with natural abilities. This is certainly true to some degree. Others say leadership can be learned.

The truth is that anybody can develop leadership ability beyond his or her current level. A good analogy for this is muscular strength and development. Certainly some people are born with more robust physiques than others, but every person has the potential and ability to work on that God-given physique to strengthen and tone the muscles. No matter how big or small, how strong or weak, every individual can work to improve his or her condition.

The leadership-development process begins by finding a source of leadership and wisdom in a particular area of interest. Training and growth begin by associating with those who have reached the "fruit on the tree." Would-be leaders should look to where the fruit hangs on the tree and then learn from those who have obtained results. Author Stevenson Willis wrote, "Seek...the counsel of those who have achieved the goal for which you strive; for in all matters, the words of one who has prospered are far weightier than the words of one who has not."

We will discuss this in more detail later in the workbook. At this point suffice it to say that leadership can and must be developed, and it occurs deliberately at the direction of someone who is already accomplished in that area. That is both the right way and the shortest way to develop leadership ability.

Leadership ability can be _____.

Do you think most people believe you have to be a "born leader"?

_____

Has anyone ever surprised you with his or her leadership abilities?

_____

_____

_____

Over the years, have you been able to grow in different areas of influence in your life? If so, which ones?

_____

_____

_____

Art and Science

The essence of leadership cannot easily be classified or codified or served up in some ready-to-order fashion. We believe the reason for this difficulty lies in the very makeup of leadership itself. You see, there are those who claim that leadership is an "art." In *Leaders on Leadership,* Doug Murren says, "A leader is more of an artist than a scientist or a politician; leadership itself is an art form." Being an art, it would come easily to people with the right "talent." Others claim there is no art to being a great leader and that it is entirely learnable. Still others split these claims down the middle, observing that good leadership is part art and part science. We agree with this middle road. It is difficult to define exactly what a leader is, but we recognize a good one when he or she shows up!

So leadership is part *art* and part *science*. This means that leadership involves "presuppositions," which are the thought processes, mind-sets, or mentalities upon which a leader operates. This is the "art" side of leadership. Resting atop those mentalities is the "science" side, or what leaders actually "do." These are the actions and strategies of leadership. Together, blending art and science, we begin to get a picture of what leadership really is. According to author James Strock, "Leadership, built on the hard ground of truth, also requires artistry to reach the summit."

Just as both artists and scientists can develop their abilities, so too can leaders develop theirs: hence the purpose of this workbook.

The following chapters seek to help you in developing as a leader. We will begin with some prerequisites that all leaders must have before advancing and then discuss the overall Cycle of Achievement that serves as a feedback loop the leader will experience while in pursuit of growth. The workbook will crescendo to a finale with the Five Levels of Leadership.

Leadership is part _____ and part _____.

In which side of leadership do you think you are currently more capable—the mentality (art) or the doing (science) part of leadership?

_____

_____

_____

WHAT A LEADER BRINGS

CHAPTER 2

Foundational Qualities

Study while others are sleeping; work while others are loafing; prepare while others are playing; and dream while others are wishing.

—William A. Ward

The journey into the center of this concept called leadership has only just begun. Everything we've discussed so far can be thought of as a road map, one that provided guidance to the location where an understanding of leadership can be discovered. Arriving in that place, we must next open a door to a structure that presents leadership as a series of ascending stairs. Gaining access to the base of those stairs is what this chapter is all about. Before anyone can begin ascending the stairs of leadership success, he or she must possess the correct combination to open the door.

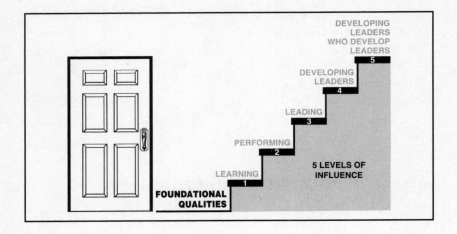

This combination to entry is comprised of the Three Hs. These three characteristics of "raw material" for a leader are:

1. Hungry
2. Hone-able
3. Honorable

These are the foundational qualities of a leader, the Three Hs that must be possessed by the leader-to-be as a prerequisite to further advancement. It is futile to proceed in leadership development without these cornerstones. One cannot begin climbing the stairs until one enters the room where the staircase begins.

Foundational Quality 1: Hungry

A leader is driven to change the status quo. As we discussed in the previous chapter, a leader is not just unhappy with things as they are; he or she must also want to change them for the better. This discontent produces the ambition or motivation to press forward and strive toward change. Some call it the will to win. Author John MacArthur writes: "All gifted leaders seem to have an innate drive to win. Those who lack the winning instinct don't make very effective leaders."

In your own words, what is "the will to win"?

_____

_____

_____

When have you displayed "the will to win"?

_____

_____

_____

Hunger itself is one of the biggest facets of leadership. Hunger provides the energy to begin, the stamina to persist, and the will to finish an endeavor. It is this hunger or ambition that births leadership. Leadership is not determined by one's birth, as they believed in Europe in the Middle Ages, nor is it determined by one's position, as many believe today; but rather, it is determined by influence and performance. Hunger is its cause.

There is an equation that is analogous to this very idea of hunger:

$$Work = Force \times Distance$$

This formula represents physical entities in nature and accurately describes how they operate. The Work done is a result of the Force multiplied by the Distance over which that Force functions. In the case of leadership, the Work done can be looked upon as the Results. The Force would be the Effort expended by the leader and his followers, and the Distance could be considered the Scope or

Reach of the leadership over time or over people. Applying leadership terminology, then, to a law of physics, we would get:

$$\text{Results or Influence} = \text{Effort} \times \text{Scope or Reach}$$

We can see that Effort plays a vital role. Effort is the direct result of the hunger involved, and the greater the Effort, the greater the Results or Influence. If an individual is only marginally committed to achieving a certain goal, it is more than likely that the goal will never be accomplished. The Effort must be significant, and significant efforts come only from those who are significantly "hungry."

The legend is told of a young squire in the service of a great knight. The squire's lifelong ambition is to someday become a knight himself. Through the years, the knight trains the squire in techniques of battle and weaponry. Being young, the squire is impatient and is prone to ask the knight if he, the squire, is ready to officially become a knight yet. Tiring of these repeated questions, the great knight sends his squire high into the hills to seek out an old sage who had once been the greatest knight of all. After a long and arduous journey, the young squire finds the sage.

"I have been sent by my liege to seek your counsel. He has told me you can determine when I shall be worthy to become a knight."

The sage answers with silence but motions for the boy to follow him to the shore of a large mountain lake. Quietly, they set out in a small boat until they reach the very center of the water.

"Submerge yourself in the water," commands the mysterious sage to the squire.

"Jump in?" asks the squire.

The sage simply nods. The squire leaps from the boat into the frigid mountain spring water. But before the boy can reemerge, the sage reaches into the water and grabs the squire's head, holding him under. The squire kicks furiously and grabs at the still strong arm of the sage, but to no avail. The seconds drag into minutes, and finally the fight is all but gone out of the squire. At that instant, the sage lifts the boy back into the boat.

Furious, gasping, fearful, and exhausted, the squire looks up at the sage.

"Why were you trying to kill me?"

"I wasn't. If I had tried to kill you, I would have succeeded."

"What were you doing, then?" asks the squire incredulously.

"Teaching you."

"Some lesson! What exactly was I supposed to learn—that you're a crazy old coot?"

"Aye, that and more," the sage nods serenely. "Let me ask you a question. When I had you submerged, what was going through your mind?"

The squire thinks a moment, his anger subsiding a bit.

"Air, I thought. Air. I've got to get air, or I'll die. That's all I was thinking."

"There you have it, then, young squire. When you want to be a knight as badly as you wanted that air, you'll become one."

This little story is an accurate depiction of what we might call "significant hunger." Certainly the squire was motivated by the threat on his own life. Although the story provides an illustration through an exaggeration, the moral is nonetheless clear.

Why do you think the wise old sage didn't just talk to the young squire to see if he was ready to become a knight?

_____

_____

_____

Have you ever wanted something as much as you want air? Explain.

_____

_____

_____

To accomplish anything lofty, you must be significantly motivated. A visual way to represent ambition or hunger is as follows:

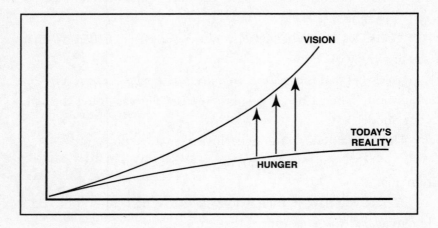

On this chart, today's reality is the bottom curve, and the leader's vision of a better reality is the top curve. The gap between the two is hunger. This graph clearly shows that hunger grows as a seed in the soil of discontent and stretches upward toward a better vision of tomorrow like a plant toward the sun.

By increasing your vision, you are able to increase your _____, which increases your efforts and increases your results.

Do you agree that the hunger to achieve a certain goal is critical to leadership?

_____

What would happen if a leader did not have much hunger or a will to win?

_____

_____

_____

Hunger as a Discipline

Those who take active responsibility to foster their motivation on a regular basis will outperform those who do not. It is the responsibility of the leader to keep him or herself hungry on a regular basis. Napoleon Hill, author of the world-famous book *Think and Grow Rich*, said, "One must realize that all who have accumulated great fortunes first did a certain amount of dreaming, hoping, wishing, desiring, and planning *before* they acquired money."

All of leadership starts with hunger. At any point in time when the leader is not hungry, the leader is not functioning as a leader. This may sound radical, but it is true. Remember, a leader takes people somewhere. The moment the leader is not moving, the leader is not leading. And it takes ambition to keep the leader moving.

Picture success as a road that leads to your dreams:

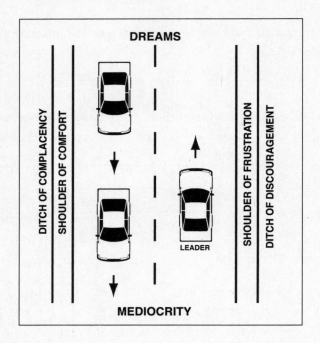

Along each side of the road are shoulders. Often the shoulders of roads are comprised of gravel. If a driver inadvertently runs onto the gravel, the sound serves as a warning that a course correction is required to resume traveling safely on the road. Conversely, sometimes that same gravel can grip the wheels of the vehicle and pull it from the road into the ditch.

On the left shoulder is *comfort*. Comfort is fine in small doses and in certain areas of life, but, like gravel, it can also serve as a warning. Remember, ambition flourishes in discontent with the status quo. Discontent and comfort cannot coexist. If a leader becomes too comfortable, ambition will die, and the soft gravel of comfort can pull him or her down into the Ditch of Complacency. Complacency pulls a leader from the road of success and halts all travel toward his or her dreams, as when a car is stuck in a ditch.

There is another danger in traveling too close to the Shoulder of Comfort: opposing traffic. Most people in life are looking for the easy road. They want comfort and will pay the price of mediocrity to get it, so they rush toward it like cows to the barn at feeding time. If a leader attempts to lead from a position of comfort, he or she will run smack into that mass of traffic heading in the other direction away from dreams and toward mediocrity. Leaders, however, shun comfort and seek excellence instead.

Also notice that being a leader means traveling close to the Shoulder of Frustration. In fact, this is the mark of any true leader. Being a leader is a study in managed frustration. How can one have ambition for a brighter tomorrow without being frustrated with the current set of realities? How can a leader be at war with the status quo and not be frustrated at the same time? The answer, of course, is that no leader can. Frustration can be healthy, but, just like the shoulder on the other side of the road, this gravel of frustration presents a trap. Too much frustration can be a warning to the leader that his or her attitude is dipping and could pull the leader down into the Ditch of Discouragement. Discouragement is a showstopper because it robs the leader of hope. Without hope, the leader is trapped in the Ditch of Discouragement and makes no further progress toward his or her dreams.

The only way to stay away from oncoming traffic, the Shoulder of Comfort, and the Ditch of Complacency—and the only way to travel near the Shoulder of Frustration but clear of the Ditch of Discouragement—is to focus straight ahead on the dreams in front of you. Having a dream-focus keeps a leader safely on the Road to Success. The best way to stay focused is to manage that hunger.

All of leadership starts with _____.

Being a leader is a study in managed _____.

Why is a small dose of frustration a good thing?

_____

_____

_____

Staying hungry, then, is actually a discipline. Many times, leaders don't need to know more about *what* is to be done; they need to find more leverage for themselves to do what they already know how to do. How, exactly, is this done?

The Three Levels of Motivation

There are Three Levels of Motivation where hunger is fed and nurtured. The first is not quite as powerful as the second, and the second is not quite as powerful as the third.

Motivation Level 1: Material Success

This first category is comprised of all the material things that excite our senses and stimulate us to want to perform. For many people, one of the attractive aspects of performing as a leader in their field is the material or financial gain that can accompany that success. One doesn't have to look far or long for "things" that are desirable. Our modern commercial society is full of entertainments, trappings, rewards, and enticements that require money. Some people like nice cars and dream of buying that new convertible with the leather interior and sporty wheels. Others dream of building their own custom home suited to their exact specifications, perhaps on a nice remote parcel of land. Still others desire travel to exotic locations where they can meet interesting new people and sample regional cuisine. Attending professional sporting events in boxed seats, having enough money to alleviate debts, developing financial security, or retiring early are all common dreams. These and an endless list of other material rewards can and should be stimulating. The excitement about earning enough money to make these dreams a reality can serve as a level of motivation and fuel ambition. Author and speaker Anthony Robbins tells us, "If you get a big enough why, you can always figure out the how."

What are some material successes that get you excited? If you had unlimited resources, what would you set out to accomplish?

_____

_____

_____

If all cars cost only $1, what kinds would you buy? Be specific (model, color, year, options, etc.).

1. _____
2. _____
3. _____
4. _____
5. _____

If you could travel anywhere and stay as long as you wanted, where would you go?

1. _____
2. _____
3. _____
4. _____
5. _____

Describe your dream home (style, size, location, land, etc.).

1. _____
2. _____
3. _____
4. _____
5. _____

What other "toys" (boats, vehicles, guns, gadgets, clothes, accessories, etc.) do you want?

1. _____
2. _____
3. _____
4. _____
5. _____

How much money do you want in your savings account?

_____

How old do you want to be when you are able to retire?

_____

How much debt do you want to have?

_____

Fill in these last lines with other dreams. Feel free to write more on another piece of paper.

1. _____
2. _____
3. _____
4. _____
5. _____

Spend time "dream building" with friends and family. Go out and see, touch, smell, and experience all your different dreams. Test-drive the above cars. Tour through homes and properties like the ones you described. Look at brochures and online pictures of all your dreams. Create a dream/vision board, full of pictures of your dreams and goals, and place it somewhere in your home where you will see it frequently. Not only can these things be a lot of fun, but you'll alert all your senses and get your subconscious mind working full force toward success. Your hunger level will continue to rise.

CONTRIBUTION AND CHARITABLE GIVING

A discussion on motivation at this level would be incomplete without pointing out that "material reward" can also provide for increased charitable giving. This is an exciting category for everyone who has causes that touch his or her heart. Perhaps one is concerned about the plight of the homeless in our land, or starving children in foreign countries, or those in crisis pregnancies, or battered wives, or orphaned children, or the severely disabled. Maybe there is a concern about the three little children down the road whose parents don't have enough money for Christmas. Perhaps one would like to donate money to a church for its outreach or missions programs. These causes all require two things: people who care and money. Familiarizing oneself with the needs of others is a very important form of dream building.

What charities do you want to help?

_____

_____

_____

What family members or friends would you like to help?

_____

_____

_____

To which other causes would you like to give more time and money?

_____

_____

_____

Negative Motivations

Level 1 motivation is not always driven by positive rewards. It can also spring from negative realities. Anthony Robbins talks about the equally motivational forces of pain and pleasure.

Still speaking of material issues, we can see how a lack of money could be a motivator. Others are motivated to achieve more success because they have a significant lack of time to spend with friends or family and in community service. Some are so oppressed by debt and negative cash flow that they are sufficiently motivated. They are sick of borrowing from Peter to pay Paul and even at times getting all the apostles involved! The warning here, however, is not to dwell on these negative motivators too much. We would never want to induce depression! Clinical studies have proven that depression is not motivating.

What are some negative things in your life that extra time and money would be able to solve?

_____

_____

_____

Motivation Level 2: Recognition and Respect

The next level of motivation is comprised of recognition and respect. This is a deeper, more powerful level than that of material success.

RECOGNITION

It is a fact that many people don't feel appreciated. Most crave the recognition that others can provide; a part of human nature is a deep need to be noticed and appreciated by others. Perhaps one wishes to accomplish a level of achievement in business or at work because it drives public recognition. Maybe one wants the title that accompanies more responsibility at work or desires to win the plaque or trophy that is coveted in that field. These and other forms of recognition can and should be used as motivations for performance, as long as one's need for affirmation from others does not grow too strong. Alas, as with all things, there are limits.

How do you feel when others show you genuine appreciation?

_____

_____

_____

When was the last time you showed someone genuine appreciation?

_____

_____

_____

What level of achievement at work or in your business would make you feel more like a success?

_____

_____

_____

RESPECT

There is, however, a deeper level to this category of motivation. That deeper level is called respect. Much stronger than the need for simple recognition is the desire for somebody you respect to give respect in return.

Perhaps one wishes for a peer group at work or in business to notice and respect his or her accomplishments. Many people are motivated to obtain the respect of a mentor, parent, teacher, or boss. Still others seek the respect of their spouses. And at perhaps the deepest level in this category, there are those who are fighting for self-respect.

Another category of respect could be called "silencing the critics." The motivational aspects of this one are easy to see. How many ambitious performers have been stifled with criticism? How many of the great figures of history have had bellicose critics who cursed them at every turn? The answer? Almost all!

Henry Ford was called "greasy fingers." Benjamin Franklin was first criticized by colonists for being too European and then by Europeans for becoming a champion in the cause of liberty for the colonies. Of Fred Astaire it was said, "Can't act. Can't sing. Slightly bald. Can dance a little." A Hollywood agent said of Lucille Ball, "Don't pay any attention to her. She's great at parties, but I can't see any future for her in movies." The manager of the Grand Ole Opry told Elvis Presley, "You ain't going nowhere; you ought to go back to driving a truck!" The Munich Technical Institute said of a young applicant named Albert Einstein, "Shows no promise."

Criticism is a fact of life for any performer, and it can be a great motivator to have someone telling you that you can't or shouldn't accomplish something. But, once again, don't take this too far. Chances are that no matter what you accomplish, you will not receive respect from critics. Why? Because giving respect is not their job. They are critics. If they ever stop criticizing, then by definition, they cease being critics; they cease to exist. And nobody wants to cease to exist. So go ahead and perform. Prove the critics wrong. Use their doubts and negativism as a great motivator. *But look only to those you respect for respect.* Ignore the critics. Or better yet, look at criticism as a sign that you are on the right track!

A small warning: One should never become overly concerned with seeking the approval of other people. Ultimately, their approval or denial is something over which we have no control. As a leader, seek the approval of successful people who have set a good example and who care about you and your success. This can be accomplished in a productive way when things are kept in balance.

Finally, and second only to pleasing God, pursue self-respect.

Look only to those you respect for _____.

Whom do you respect? Why is it important for you to receive respect in return from that person?

_____

_____

_____

Are there critics whom you'd like to prove wrong?

_____

_____

_____

Motivation Level 3: Purpose, Destiny, and Legacy

PURPOSE

Material reward and contribution are exciting. Recognition and respect can be even bigger drivers, but by far, the most sustaining, important, deep, and durable motivation comes from a sense of purpose. Purpose is the "true north" for our mental and emotional inner compass. Purpose takes us out of the realm of living only for ourselves and our own selfish desires and onto a higher plane. Purpose involves sacrifice for a greater good, contribution for making a bigger difference, and energies directed at a long-term view.

It has been said that "our purpose in life is to find a purpose in life." We are here for a reason. Our birth and development were not by mistake or the result of a series of cosmic accidents of chance.

Viktor Frankl said, "We do not determine our purpose; we detect it." One man likened this process of discovery to unearthing an important archeological artifact. The scientist carefully removes small layers of soil from the find. As the time-consuming process progresses, more and more of the artifact becomes visible and more and more can be learned about it, until the entire object is fully unearthed and displayed to the world. Individually, our purposes in life are a lot like that. We may feel for years as though we are digging for it. This can often be a slow and painstaking process. But, sticking to the search, eventually we start to uncover small bits and pieces of what God has built and equipped us to do. As we explore further, our purpose becomes clearer. And, hopefully, if we work diligently toward answers, the full purpose is disclosed and enthusiastically embraced. This is vitally important. As General Douglas MacArthur said, "Every man should be embarrassed to die until he accomplishes something great in this world."

Our purpose in life is to find _____ _____
_____ _____.

We are here for _____ _____.

We do not determine our purpose; we _____
_____.

Have you detected your purpose(s) in life yet? If so, what have you found?

_____

_____

_____

DESTINY

Destiny takes purpose further, comprehending the spiritual component. Destiny says that we were created, created for a purpose, and the unique abilities and opportunities that we find in our lives are God-given. Who you are, where you live, the talents you were born with, and the opportunities that have and will come your way are all part of a bigger picture, a picture into which you were painted to fulfill a part that only you can.

You may find this hard to accept, thinking that perhaps life is a bundle of chance occurrences. We understand such skepticism and respect the right of people have to it. But as our good friend Tim Marks says, "Be sure you know why you believe what you believe." Our study of history has shown again and again that, as Benjamin Franklin said at the Constitutional Convention that shaped our nation, "God governs in the affairs of men."

William H. Murray said, "The moment one definitely commits oneself, then Providence moves too. All sorts of things occur to help one that would never otherwise have occurred. A whole stream of events issue from the decision, raising in one's favor all manner of unforeseen incidents and meetings and material assistance which no man could have dreamed would come his way." Talk about possibility thinking! It's the "Providence moves too" concept that we are examining here. What could be more motivating than to know that what you are doing is destined, that you are supposed to do it, and that Providence moves to help you?

Destiny is the deepest level of motivation available. Understanding it can be the most motivating, stimulating, sustaining force on your life's efforts. Respect it, nourish it, meditate on it, pray about it, and pursue it. After all, it's your destiny! May you live to fulfill it every day!

Destiny says that we were created for _____ _____.

Be sure you know _____ you _____ what you _____.

The moment one definitely _____ oneself, then _____ _____ _____.

Are you sure you know why you believe what you believe?

_____

_____

_____

What are some beliefs about your destiny that you know for sure?

_____

_____

_____

LEGACY

The Bible teaches, "It is appointed unto men once to die" (Hebrews 9:27), and not one of us can avoid it. And when that time comes, what did our life mean? What did we accomplish? What did we contribute? How will we be remembered? Who will care? When the funeral is over and the relatives are back at the church eating potato salad on rickety tables, what will they be saying?

Legacy is the answer to these questions. Whether what we do is positive, giving, and serving of other people, or destructive, selfish, and hurtful to other people, we will leave a legacy. And it is never too soon or too late to begin thinking about the legacy we're erecting with the daily living of our lives. Having an overarching purpose, understanding our personal destiny, and being truthful to it are the best components of a worthy legacy. As one famous quote states, "My life is my message."

What do you want people to say at your funeral?

_____

_____

_____

What legacies have your ancestors left?

_____

_____

_____

What do you want your posterity to do and say when they turn to *your* page in the family history book?

_____

_____

_____

What does your organization's potential legacy look like? Who is involved in building that legacy?

_____

_____

_____

Why is your organization important?

_____

_____

_____

The Three Levels of Motivation Reconsidered

There is another way to consider these Three Levels of Motivation. The shallowest motivation would consist of Success, which embodies material rewards and respect from others. The next, deeper level of motivation would be Significance, which embodies destiny and perhaps leaving a legacy. The deepest, most empowering form of motivation would be Obedience and Sacrifice to a God-given vision.

We introduce this delineation to illustrate yet another way the concept of progressive levels of motivation can be described. However, the semantics don't really matter. What does matter is that would-be leaders understand the importance of hunger in its various forms and how to discover it, stoke its flames, and fan it into a blazing inferno. Leaders must cultivate all three of these sources of motivation on a regular basis to fuel performance and sustain it over the long haul.

Every action one takes is either one step closer or one step farther from his or her destiny. Remember, many begin the journey. Very few finish well. It's the *hungry* who make it.

Are you hungry to grow as a leader yet? If not, continue working on your Three Levels of Motivation. The rest of this workbook will be a waste of time if you don't have a burning desire to grow and change.

Foundational Quality 2: Hone-able

The definition of hone is "to sharpen or smooth with a whetstone or to make more acute, intense, or effective." The second foundational quality of a leader is to be hone-able, to have an attitude that allows intensifying and sharpening.

The great Socrates stated that if he was the wisest man in Athens, it could only be because he alone assumed he didn't have all the answers. The point is that when it comes to learning, we should never assume we have arrived. For a leader there is no completion to education. We need to live like we will die tomorrow and learn like we will live forever. When a leader remains teachable, his or her potential is limitless. With this in mind, there are several roadblocks to learning that a leader must constantly avoid.

We need to live like we will die _____ and learn like we will live _____.

Arrogance

Being teachable is as much an attitude as anything else. The "know-it-all" attitude is the death warrant of achievement. In the words of F. A. Hayek, "Nothing is more securely lodged than the ignorance of the experts." A true leader knows that no matter how much he has achieved, he still has more to learn.

The opposite of arrogance is humility. Most important, this means being humble toward mentors (more on this in later chapters), peers, and subordinates. Leaders can learn from anyone in any position and should have a humble attitude that allows learning to take place.

A true leader knows that no matter how much he has _____, he still has more to _____.

Have you encountered the "know-it-all" type? Do you have a "know-it-all" attitude? How have you noticed this attitude hindering progress and success?

_____

_____

_____

Disinterest

A leader must be sincerely interested in learning more on a regular basis. Disinterest or apathy will lead to outdated knowledge and poor decision making. Neither of these can exist for long without fatal results in the life of a leader's endeavors.

Disinterest or _____ will lead to outdated _____ and poor decision making.

Do you know someone who has been stopped by the roadblock of disinterest? If so, how have you noticed this hindering the person?

_____

_____

_____

Wrong Assumptions

A leader may be open and interested in learning but still blinded by wrong assumptions. Sometimes those closest to a situation cannot see something that is obvious to a fresh set of eyes. As President Ronald Reagan was fond of saying to Soviet premier Mikhail Gorbachev, "Trust, but verify." Leaders must have open and inquisitive minds and be slow to jump to conclusions based on previous assumptions.

"Trust, but _____."

Do you know someone who has been stopped by the roadblock of wrong assumptions? If so, how have you noticed this hindering the person?

_____

_____

_____

Entrenched Habits

We are all a product of our habits. Habits can be good, and they can be damaging. However, what every leader must take care to avoid is leading by habit, never learning anything new, and just doing what he has always done in the manner he has always done it. Such a leader is no longer a leader, but a manager. Entrenched habits that prohibit the process of learning are poison. "That's just the way we've always done it," should never be said by any leader at any time or any place.

Habits can be _____, and they can be _____.

Do you know someone who has been stopped by the roadblock of entrenched habits? If so, how have you noticed this hindering the person?

_____

_____

_____

Not-Invented-Here Syndrome

Not-Invented-Here (NIH) syndrome could actually be considered a form of arrogance. When a leader resists learning something new because it wasn't her idea, that leader's educational process is sacrificed on the altar of her pride. Good ideas can and usually do come from everywhere. Great leaders accept and embrace that fact and strive to learn all they can, no matter whose idea began the process. A leader should be open to learning about new ideas, no matter the source.

Good ideas can and usually do come from _____.

Do you know someone who has been stopped by the roadblock of NIH syndrome? If so, how have you noticed this hindering the person?

_____

_____

_____

Wrong Priorities

Sometimes a leader may have a healthy attitude about learning but still misses the mark by misunderstanding priorities. This usually occurs when the leader is busy doing the wrong things. Leaders must live in the realm of the *important*, not in the realm of the *urgent*.

Usually it works like this: A leader begins investing time in important issues and then gets interrupted by urgent issues. Gradually, the urgent issues eat away the time the leader has to spend working on important issues. The more this happens, the more urgent issues erupt because the important things are not being handled. Eventually, the leader is engulfed by urgent crises and has no time for important, vital issues at all.

Busyness due to wrong priorities is a very common roadblock to the teachability of a leader. Every leader must be aware of this and not let the day-to-day pull of responsibility eclipse his ability to learn and grow.

Leaders must live in the realm of the _____, not in the realm of the *urgent*.

Do you know someone who has been stopped by the roadblock of wrong priorities? If so, how have you noticed this hindering the person?

_____

_____

_____

Cynicism

As with many of these roadblocks to learning, cynicism has much to do with attitude. It can be defined as "the condition of being contemptuously distrustful of human nature and motives." Cynicism is what happens when skepticism is given too much latitude. A small dose of skepticism is healthy in a leader and provides a buffer against gullible mistakes, but if skepticism is allowed to warp a leader's perspective, cynicism is the product.

Leaders approach situations and challenges with a learner's mind-set, that is, as a student and not as a critic. Leaders must approach learning with a positive, curious inquisitiveness and never allow their responsibilities or setbacks to sour their disposition.

Leaders approach situations and challenges as a _____ and not as a critic.

Do you know someone who has been stopped by the roadblock of cynicism? If so, how have you noticed this hindering the person?

_____

_____

_____

A leader must diligently avoid each of the above roadblocks to learning and fight to remain teachable. To be an unteachable leader is to be a leader headed for a crash.

Why do these roadblocks of learning seem to be so common today?

_____

_____

_____

Which of these roadblocks of learning have you had trouble with in the past?

_____

_____

_____

How did the roadblock(s) hinder you?

_____

_____

_____

How did you get past them, or how do you plan to get past them?

_____

_____

_____

Foundational Quality 3: Honorable

Integrity can be considered as the condition of "not doing what's wrong." Character can be defined as doing the right thing for the mere reason that it is the right thing, even if that thing is difficult and unpopular. The two sewn together make honor.

Honor is such a rarely used word in our times that it seems a little old-fashioned. But living a life of integrity and character is timeless and, for a leader, absolutely necessary. It's about choices, and a person's choices in life follow him to the grave.

Is this to say that a person needs to be perfect to become a leader? Of course not. Perfection in this life is not possible, and we, the authors, are certainly not exceptions. However, a leader must strive continually toward perfection even though she knows she can never attain it exactly. It is a question of the heart. If a leader cuts corners, misuses people, or misrepresents the truth, a time bomb begins ticking. Someday, somewhere, the bomb will go off. It is obvious in our times all too often: public figures at the pinnacle of power and fame crash and burn in a cloud of self-inflicted shame. From political scandals to high-profile corporate frauds, these calamities are brought on by a lack of honor in the leadership.

The difference between leaders we revile and those we praise is their individual level of honor. In fact, honor is the force that holds a leader's hunger in check. Without honor, hunger runs rampant and ultimately serves only selfish interests. Honor is the component that makes hunger productive for the leader's fellow man. In fact, what we are basically describing here is another "old-fashioned" word: duty. George Washington said of duty, "Human happiness and moral duty are inseparably connected." So leadership is spawned by hunger and held in check by honor. Under that combination, leaders will find happiness in the fulfillment of their duty to others.

This concept of honor is so important to a leader because people will follow a leader only as far as they feel they can trust him. People will not follow a leader they can't trust.

Finally, it should be remembered that a major component of honor is personal courage. Without the courage to do what's right because it's right, regardless of ramifications to self, one is not truly worthy to be called a leader.

Integrity can be understood as the behavior of "not doing _____ _____."

Character can be defined as doing the _____ thing for the mere reason that it is the _____ thing, even if that thing is _____ and _____.

A major component of honor is personal _____.

If you asked various people in your life how you're doing in the area of honor, how do think they would respond?

A) You live by high standards; your word is your worth, and your worth is your word.

B) You are consistent most of the time and easily engender trust.

C) You could stand to become more consistent in words and actions.

D) You are a mystery; people aren't sure what you believe and rarely know how you will act.

For many people, it's easy to maintain integrity in the big things. They would never engage in theft, character assassination, or fraud, but they have a hard time in the smaller things. Yet leaders need to be aware that followers watch everything leaders do. What little things do you have difficulty with?

_____

_____

_____

How do you determine your values in regard to personal honor? Where do you look for those standards?

_____

_____

_____

What are some ways to build personal courage?

_____

_____

_____

Summary

The three foundational qualities of a leader, the Three Hs, are required to gain access to leadership capability. Being hungry, honeable, and honorable are required to open the door to the base of the stairs of leadership success.

WHAT A LEADER DOES

CHAPTER 3

The Cycle of Achievement

What counts is not the number of hours you put in, but how much you put in the hours.

—ANONYMOUS

With the foundational qualities in place, the leadership-development process can begin. According to Bill George in *Authentic Leadership*, "Although we may be born with leadership potential, all of us have to develop ourselves to become good leaders."

The leadership-development process is where a leader begins the work that he or she is about and uses that experience to gain ability and understanding. It is this work that propels the leader up the ascending levels of influence. This

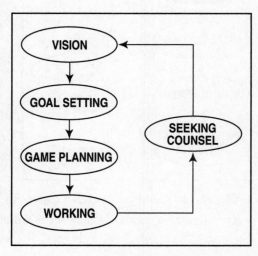

occurs according to the Cycle of Achievement, as shown in the diagram above.

As George Barna, author of *A Fish Out of Water*, said, "Leaders do the right things for the right reasons at the right times." This is not as easy as it may sound. To become capable of such performance, leaders must evolve, and they must do so deliberately. Repeatedly rotating through the Cycle of Achievement compels the leader to grow in ability, understanding, experience, discernment, and wisdom.

"Leaders do the _____ _____ for the _____ _____ at the _____ _____."

Vision

The entire Cycle of Achievement begins with vision. Vision is tomorrow's reality expressed as an idea today. Leaders must first have a vision of where they desire to take themselves and their organization.

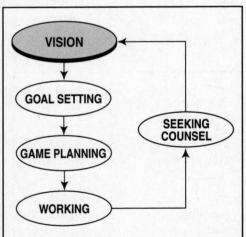

Next, leaders must cast the vision consistently before the people they influence. Vision comes from the picture of a dream in the leader's mind. One doesn't always get what one wants, and one doesn't always get what one deserves, but one *does* generally get what one *pictures*. Some call it visualization. This is where the dream-building exercise can come in handy, serving to build and maintain a clear vision in the mind of the leader.

Leaders see further than others see and then set about the process of leading followers there.

The Bible says, "Where there is no vision, the people perish" (Proverbs 29:18). Leaders supply that vision as the first step in their influence.

Vision is tomorrow's reality expressed as an _____
_____.

We generally get what we _____.

Where there is no vision, the _____
_____.

Is it possible for a person to be a leader if he or she does not possess vision?

_____

What may be lacking in the person who does not possess a clear vision?

_____

_____

_____

Think about some of the truly great leaders from history or your lifetime. Pick the one you admire most. What was his or her vision? How did the vision help that person keep going when he or she faced adversity?

_____

_____

_____

Have you been part of an organization where a strong vision was constantly being shared? If so, how did this affect the results of the organization?

_____

_____

_____

What experiences have impacted the vision you have for yourself? Your family? Your organization? (If you lack vision, how can you discover it?)

_____

_____

_____

Goal Setting

It is important to be hungry and have ambition to change the status quo, with a clear vision of what is to be, but that energy must be directed at something specific. That is where goals enter the

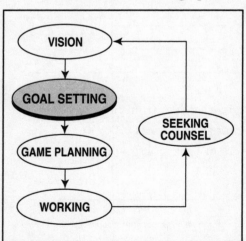

picture. David Schwartz, author of *The Magic of Thinking Big,* writes, "A goal is more than a dream; it's a dream being acted upon." Without specific goals at which to direct energies and ambitions, all efforts will be wandering generalities at best. A leader must know the goal of his or her efforts. A leader must know clearly what is to be achieved. In short, leaders use the process of goal setting.

As with hunger, goal setting is a discipline. It should never be a haphazard affair. With this in mind, there are several components to the proper setting of goals that every leader should embody.

"A goal is more than a dream; it's a dream being _____ upon."

Consider times in your work or other duties when you had a goal and when you didn't? What was the difference in your results?

_____

_____

_____

How does goal setting help with establishing priorities?

_____

_____

_____

Goals Must Be Specific

Goals must be clear and exact. Examples of proper specific goals would be "to win the Boston Marathon" or "to become president of the company" or "to sell one million dollars' worth of products this year." These are clear and precise. Examples of goals that may not be specific enough are "to become a better father" or "to improve in leadership ability" or "to maximize performance at work." These are general feelings of what could be accomplished, but terms like "better father" or "improve ability" or "maximize" are not specific enough to trap the leader into performing. How can one know if he really became a better father or improved his ability or maximized? Being specific with goals not only gives the leader a clear target at which to shoot, but it also leaves no room for doubt as to whether the target was hit. That is what it means to be specific.

Goals must be clear and _____.

Goals Must Be Written

A goal is not a goal until the leader has written it down. This may sound trite, but it is vitally important. As with goals that are not specific, goals not written down leave the leader room to maneuver if things don't go as planned. But a written goal is hard to avoid.

A goal is not a goal until the leader has _____ it down.

Do you have the habit of writing down goals, or do you just think or talk about them?

_____

_____

_____

If you aren't in the habit of writing down your goals, what can you do to change that?

_____

_____

_____

Goals Must Be Set in Stone

The purpose of having a goal in the first place is to organize a leader's thoughts and provide something specific for which to strive. The setting of a goal must be backed by commitment, or the whole process breaks down. Therefore, goals must be "set in stone." Once decided upon, goals should not be changed. There is a saying: "Goals are etched in stone, but plans are drawn in sand." As will be shown in "Game Planning," it may be necessary to modify plans for how to attain a goal, but the goal itself must remain firm. Commitment says that whether the goal is accomplished using Plan A or Plan Z, the goal remains.

"Goals are etched in _____, but plans are drawn in _____."

What can happen if you don't set a goal in stone?

_____

_____

_____

Have you ever set a goal in stone and had to change your game plan on the way toward the goal? If so, how many times did you have to change the plan before you achieved the goal?

_____

_____

_____

Goals Must Be Measurable

If a goal is to exert a motivating force upon the leader, then there must be a clear, quantifiable method to determine when the goal has been accomplished. Can it be measured? The ability to measure progress toward a goal also enables midcourse corrections and helps a leader to confront brutal reality concerning his or her progress.

Goals Must Be Realistic

If the goal is too far beyond the leader's reach, the leader will eventually become exasperated at his repeated failure to accomplish that goal. Goals must be realistic enough that the leader believes them achievable and is energized to do whatever it takes to accomplish them.

What is the difference between having a big dream/vision and a having a realistic goal?

_____

_____

_____

Have you set a goal before that was not realistic? Were you able to hit it? Have you given up on a goal because it seemed too far away or too difficult?

_____

_____

_____

Goals Must Provide Motivation

On one hand, goals must be realistic, but on the other, they must be enough of a stretch to inspire the leader. They must be challenging. They must cause discomfort on the part of the leader and provide an impetus for increased performance.

What goals have you had in the past that were exciting or motivating?

_____

_____

_____

What about these goals made them exciting?

_____

_____

_____

What goals have you had in the past that were *not* exciting or motivating?

_____

_____

_____

Why were they *not* exciting or motivating?

_____

_____

_____

What were the biggest differences between the motivating goals and the non-motivating ones?

_____

_____

_____

Have you ever been forced to grow your abilities in order to accomplish a goal? If so, what was the goal, and which abilities did you have to grow?

_____

_____

_____

Goals Must Be in Line with Priorities and Values

In the struggle for achievement, there will always be temptations to "sell out" or compromise one's beliefs. There may be conflicts of interest that crop up along the way, but under no circumstances whatsoever should a leader set goals that don't ring true with her true priorities and values in life. As the verse says, "For what shall it profit a man, if he shall gain the whole world, and lose his own soul?" (Mark 8:36). Every leader should take care when setting goals to ensure that the goal itself is not at cross purposes with her core beliefs, nor that what's required to accomplish the goal compromises her honor.

"For what shall it profit a man, if he shall gain the whole _____ and lose his own _____?"

Goals Must Be Prominent

The leader must develop systematic ways of regularly reminding himself of the goal. This can be done with signs or placards placed around the home or workplace or even in the car. This may mean telling a spouse or friend or work associate about the goal so he or she can continue to bring it up in conversation. (This step should be done cautiously, however. The Bible warns against "casting your pearls before swine" [Matthew 7:6], which means be careful with whom you share your most cherished thoughts, including personal goals. Sharing of goals should be done only with the closest of trusted individuals.) A goal forgotten is a goal missed. Great leaders know to put pressure on themselves by developing creative reminders of their commitments to achievement.

Where can you place your written goals so you can constantly see them?

_____

_____

_____

Name three possible people (mentors, coaches, friends, your spouse, etc.) in whom you can confide your goals and who will hold you accountable.

1. _____

2. _____

3. _____

Why did you choose these people?

_____

_____

_____

What about them has earned your trust?

_____

_____

_____

Goals Must Have a Specific Time Period

If a goal is set without a time limit, it becomes nothing more than a wish or fantasy. A time limit applies the final pressure on the leader, like a clock ticking during the running of a race. The pressure of the clock is necessary to avoid the old saying, "When all is said and done, there is usually more said than done!"

If a goal is set without a _____ _____,
it becomes nothing more than a _____ or
_____.

Have you ever played a sport where there was no exact time period
given? Have you also played a sport when the score was tied with
only minutes left or when you were down to the last inning? What
was the difference in your and your team's attitude, focus, and level
of skill applied?

_____

_____

_____

Game Planning

With these nine details of goal setting in place, the leader is focused, supercharged, and ready to perform—almost.

Referencing the Cycle of Achievement diagram once again, we
see that there is another step before the work begins that ensures
that the work leads directly to the accomplishment of the goal:

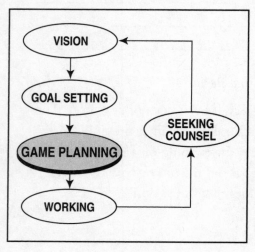

formulating a game plan. A
leader with a goal but no
game plan is like an archer
with a target and no arrows.
A game plan is a leader's
strategy or map. It provides
guidance toward the goal. It
provides the very way to realize the goal. It is here that the
leader's creative powers can
flourish. It is here that a
leader develops the ability to

think strategically, brainstorming on the methods of attack. It is here that experience and learning can be big enablers. If Hunger provides the "why," the Goal is the "what," and the Game Plan is the "how."

Try to find a coach or mentor, someone who has accomplished your goal or a similar one, to advise you on your game plan. Who might be some possible guides?

1. _____

2. _____

3. _____

Game Plans Are Set in Sand

Strategic thinking is important, and putting together a well-thought-out plan for accomplishing a goal is vital. But a leader must never allow the game plan to become a masterpiece of its own. The game plan must be fluid, adaptable to changing conditions, and able to be scrapped at a moment's notice if it's not working. As mentioned above, often it is necessary for a leader to develop multiple game plans over time before a goal can be reached. The goal is set in stone; the plan is drawn in sand.

The goal is set in _____; the plan is drawn in _____.

Game Plans Drive the Prioritization of Tasks

One of the biggest advantages of a game plan is that it drives the process of setting priorities. A leader must think through and understand the question: What's important next?

A teacher sought to demonstrate for his students the impact of prioritizing work. He took a glass jar and placed it on the desk next to some large rocks, some smaller rocks, some pebbles, some sand,

and a pitcher of water. He informed the class that the object of the exercise was to fit as many of the materials on the desk into the glass jar as possible, providing the densest combination. He first placed as many of the large rocks into the glass jar as would fit, asking the class to confirm that the jar was "full." Next, he placed the smaller rocks into the jar around the larger rocks until the class verified once again that no more rocks could be placed into the jar. Then he crammed the pebbles into the jar around the other rocks until no more would fit. Next, he poured the sand around the various-sized rocks until no more would go into the jar. Finally, he poured the pitcher of water into the sand in the jar until the jar was entirely full of matter and not one more thing would fit.

"Now the jar is full," said the teacher. "If we had not prioritized what should be placed into the jar first, we would not have fit as many of the items into the jar, and we would not have obtained the densest result."

"I don't get it," said a student. "How does that teach priorities?" "Because," answered the patient instructor, "if we had started with the smaller items such as water or sand, there would have been no room for the larger rocks. The projects we encounter in life must be handled in the same way. Put the big rocks in first. Then work downward toward the smaller things."

That is the lesson of priorities. Game planning for a leader is the step where prioritization takes place. Without it, the leader will spend time on things that are "good" to do or even "great" to do, but not the "best" to do. A leader knows to put in the "big rocks" first.

Ed Koch, author of *The 80/20 Principle*, writes, "The 80/20 Principle asserts that a minority of causes, inputs, or effort usually leads to a majority of the results, outputs, or rewards. Taken literally, this means that, for example, 80 percent of what you achieve in your job comes from 20 percent of the time spent. Thus for all practical purposes, four-fifths of the effort—a dominant part of it—is largely irrelevant." Over time, the leader's ability in this area compounds toward excellence or devolves toward mediocrity.

Do you agree with the 80/20 Principle (also called the Pareto Principle) that 20 percent of your efforts produce 80 percent of your results? Explain.

_____

_____

_____

How do you currently prioritize your responsibilities?

_____

_____

_____

How do you fill your calendar? (Hint: If you don't have one, you should get one.)

_____

_____

_____

Answer the following questions by referring to your calendar:

What is required of me?

_____

_____

_____

What gives the greatest return?

_____

_____

_____

What brings the greatest reward?

_____

_____

_____

What tasks that do not bring a high return can I delegate to someone else?

_____

_____

_____

What tasks that do not bring a high return can be stopped altogether?

_____

_____

_____

What are some of my top (20 percent) priorities?

_____

_____

_____

Game Plans Are Developed at the Macro, Mini, and Micro Levels

A close relative to the topic of prioritization is the classification of tasks or objectives into different levels based upon their size or importance. It is helpful for a leader to understand that issues can be classified into at least three categories. These are:

1. Macro
2. Mini
3. Micro

The Macro level is the overall top layer. It is comprised of all the big stuff, the high-priority stuff, or the issues that will have the biggest impact for a given task. The Mini level is just below Macro, where issues are smaller and not quite as important. Finally, the Micro level is the tiniest, detail level, where the issues are the smallest. It is important to understand how Macro, Mini, and Micro fit together with the idea of priorities discussed above.

The diagram below shows how a leader has a set of priorities that are arranged according to the principle of "What's important next?" Associated with each of these priorities are macro, mini, and micro issues. These two concepts together show the leader exactly where to focus to have the highest impact on reaching the goal. A truly effective leader structures a game plan that starts with the highest priority task and the macro issues associated with that task. As these are completed, the leader works on the next lower-priority tasks and on issues related to those tasks that go from macro down to micro.

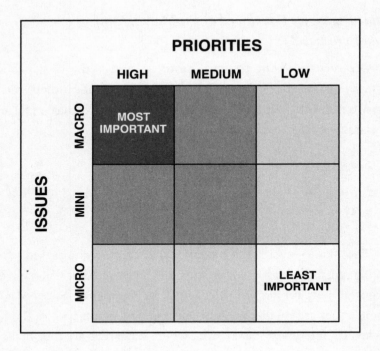

It should be noted that this chart is only one way to classify the work a leader must accomplish. It is rarely necessary that all the priorities be handled or all the issues worked out. Often a goal can be reached before that level of detail is necessary. For this reason, it is important for leaders to review their priorities and issues continually in order to have the highest impact possible as conditions change and progress is made.

Do you currently spend most of your time on macro, mini, or micro issues?

_____

_____

_____

List two high-priority macro issues you currently have.

1. _____

2. _____

List two high-priority mini issues you currently have.

1. _____

2. _____

What things might you want to temporarily give up in order to focus more time and energy toward your priorities? For example:

For six months, I will give up…

_____

_____

Instead, I will…

_____

_____

_____

My goal is to…

_____

_____

_____

I will tell _____ about my progress and ask this person to keep me accountable.

Game Plans Are Best When Effective Thinking Is Used First

A leader's quality of thinking will have much to do with that leader's success. There is tremendous power in effectively thinking through a goal and how it might be attained.

Brainstorming is the process where thinking is done in a free-wheeling style, omitting any early judgments as to the merits of the ideas that result. Evaluation of ideas can come later. Brainstorming is designed to pull all good ideas out of the head and into the game plan.

A key precept to comprehend when thinking strategically through a goal can be understood by envisioning the process like a game of dominoes. For any given goal, there are myriad tasks that lead to its accomplishment. When drawing up a game plan, the leader must ask, "What are the major dominoes that will knock all the others down?" It is critical to focus on the major tasks first. This requires forethought and planning. Once a leader has determined the steps of major importance toward the realization of a goal, all efforts should be brought to bear on the completion of those particular steps. Often people miss this point and spend time and energy working on dominoes that don't knock any others down. At the end of the time frame, the goals have gone unaccomplished and the leader is frustrated. Effective thinking leads to a proper game plan that prevents this common mistake.

A leader's quality of _____ will have much to do with that leader's _____.

Have you or someone you've observed started toward a goal without properly thinking it through? If so, what were the results and what do you think could have happened if quality thinking had gone into the game plan?

_____

_____

_____

Working

With goals set and game plans made, the leader must exert as much influence as possible toward their achievement. This is not done in a vacuum. The very definition of a leader says that other people are involved. This means that the job of the leader may seem a little less straightforward than the jobs of his subordinates. This section is designed to teach the mind-sets and attitudes of the leader's endeavors, not the details of the actual work to be done. It is meant to be as broad as possible so that leaders of all fields will find relevance for their own situations.

When applied to a leader, the term *working* encompasses several categories. Each of these is necessary in the daily actions of a leader to produce effectiveness. People will work a lot harder when they understand how their efforts fit into the bigger picture.

Working: Casting the Vision

The whole Cycle of Achievement begins with the vision of the leader, as has already been discussed. That vision must be cast and recast before the organization to make sure everybody is working in unison and understands the overall picture. People need to understand how their efforts fit into the bigger picture; it has been proven that people are much more motivated by purpose and cause than anything else. It falls to the leader, then, to be the amplifier and consistent reminder of the organization's vision.

Where does a leader's vision get its start—from within or outside the leader?

_____

_____

_____

How does a vision involve thinking "outside the lines" or "out of the box"?

_____

_____

_____

The very definition of a leader says that other people are involved. Have you tried to include others in your vision in the past? If so, how successful were you?

_____

_____

_____

How can you improve your ability to include others?

_____

_____

_____

What are some different ways of casting the vision for others?

_____

_____

_____

Working: Leading by Example

Abraham Lincoln said, "Example is not the main thing in influencing other people; it's the only thing." First and foremost, the leader sets the example.

"What you do speaks so loudly that what you say I cannot hear" points directly to the heart of the matter. Many seem to have the idea that a leader is someone with a position or someone with the ability to talk a good game. But a true leader sets the example with his or her actions on a daily basis—period.

"Example is not the _____ _____ in influencing other people; it's the _____ _____."

"What you _____ speaks so loudly that what you _____ I cannot hear."

It is said your followers will do 50 percent of what you do right and 100 percent of what you do wrong. Have you experienced this in your profession or at home? If so, explain.

_____

_____

_____

Working: Demonstrating a Strong Work Ethic

There is no shortcut to success. Leaders who search for a shortcut end up getting cut short. Although hard work is not the sole secret to success, it is certainly a critical component. Sometimes those in a position of leadership want to shirk the grunt work and instead tell others what to do, but that is not true leadership. When a leader resorts to delegating because he is not willing to do it himself, he has reverted to managing instead of leading. True leadership is being willing to live down in the trenches where the action is and do whatever is necessary.

Please don't misunderstand us here. A leader's job is not to tackle the tasks and responsibilities of his subordinates. A leader must simply be willing to, as there is no job below the leader. Peter Drucker said, "No leader is worth his salt who won't set up chairs." More importantly, though, a leader must be willing to exert himself in his own specific duties, not expecting success to come easily or cheaply. The Bible says, "…if any would not work, neither should he eat" (2 Thessalonians 3:10). When asked about the hard work involved in conducting successful scientific experiments, the great inventor Thomas Edison said, "Nothing that's good works by itself, just to please you. You've got to *make* the…thing work."

It's going to take work to become a successful leader—plain and simple. But one shouldn't despair; meaningful work can be one of life's biggest blessings. The strong work ethic demonstrated by the leader energizes the organization and propels everyone forward. As Andy Stanley said, "Courage to act defines the leader."

There is no _____ to success.

"No leader is worth his _____ who won't _____ _____ _____."

"…if any would not _____, neither should he _____."

"Courage to _____ defines the _____."

Working: Taking Responsibility

Leaders take responsibility for their actions and for their decisions. Leaders are not always right and don't always make the right decisions. Real leaders make decisions, and then they make those decisions right.

Taking responsibility means holding oneself to a standard of results. Leaders are not satisfied with being busy or with talking an issue to death. True leaders are only happy with outcomes. As the old saying goes, "If you're talking about your *effort*, then your *results* must be poor." If leaders don't like the outcomes, they make changes, taking full responsibility for implementing those changes. If something goes wrong, they take the blame. If something goes well, they share the credit. But underneath it all, the leader takes ownership and determines that "If it's to be, it's up to me!"

President Harry Truman was known for his straightforward thinking and no-nonsense approach to decision making. As a young man after World War I, Truman opened up a haberdashery with a war buddy. The business went bankrupt, but Truman accepted responsibility and paid back all the debts. Later in life, as president, Harry Truman had a sign on his desk that read "The buck stops here." Truman understood that along with leadership comes the responsibility to make tough decisions.

Leaders take responsibility—period.

"If you're talking about your _____, then your _____ must be poor."

If something goes wrong, leaders take the _____. If something goes well, leaders share the _____.

"The _____ stops _____."

Do you know of examples of "leaders" who continually blame others or circumstances for their lack of results? If so, do you notice a trend in their ability to get results?

_____

_____

Working: Orchestrating and Aligning Resources

A true leader assumes responsibility for orchestrating and aligning resources. This involves equipping others or making sure that others are adequately managing resources. The best leadership team in the world cannot function if it runs out of what it requires to operate.

Many are the stories of leaders whose grand visions failed because of a lack of resources or proper allocation thereof. Napoleon's Grand Army marched against Russia and got trapped by winter and a total lack of resupply. As the French forces advanced, the Russian forces burned and destroyed every scrap of food or crop that could be used by Napoleon's troops. As a result, an enormous army nearly disintegrated. It wasn't a lack of ability or training, nor was it a lack of a strong vision or charismatic leadership; it was a failing of resources (and ultimately, strategy). Leaders take full responsibility for the even operation of their organizations and its flow of necessary resources.

What possible resources are available in your organization?

_____

_____

_____

Working: Solving Problems and Removing Obstacles

Leaders anticipate problems or obstacles that will impede plans so they can be solved and removed before negative consequences result. This requires active mental engagement. Leaders must constantly be thinking and searching for anything that will crop up to bring catastrophe to their operations. When these things are identified, or even suspected, strategic plans must be put in place to eradicate them. The best way to deal with a problem is to attack while the problem is still small. There is no sense in chopping down a full-grown tree later when it could be plucked out as a twig today.

There are two sources of obstacles to the success of a leader's organization. The first is internal elements, and the second is outside influences. Internal obstacles are under the authority of the leader and can be addressed head-on. Fixing these requires courage, healthy confrontation, and firm fairness. External elements may or may not be changeable by the leader, but the leader must find a way to deal with the situation. Leaders who ignore outside interferences or simply hope they will eventually go away are dooming their organization to certain failure. Remember, leaders take responsibility for results. That includes results that are affected by outside factors such as the economy, the actions of a competitor, attack from special-interest groups, weather, and changes in the law. While a leader may not be able to change the conditions, he or she is responsible for success in spite of those conditions.

While a leader may not be able to _____ the conditions, he or she is responsible for success _____ _____ of those conditions.

In the past, what types of obstacles have you had to deal with that came from within your organization? How did you plan for these, or how should you have planned for these?

_____

_____

_____

What types of obstacles have you had to deal with that came from outside your organization? How did you plan for these, or how should you have planned for these?

_____

_____

_____

Working: Searching for Opportunities

Leaders have watchful eyes. They scan their world for emerging opportunities all the time. Again, both internally and externally, opportunities crop up on a regular basis. This is where the ability to assess and take risks and the ability to prioritize become critical. It is imperative that organizations take advantage of new opportunities, but not *every* opportunity. If an opportunity is in line with the vision, then leaders take their organizations in that direction; all other possibilities must be left aside. It is the job of the leader to identify, analyze, and decide which opportunities to exploit and which to ignore, all the while casting and recasting the vision so the organization accepts the new challenges wholeheartedly.

It is imperative that organizations take advantage of new _____, but not *every* _____.

Working: Being Consistent

Since the actions of a leader are the example for the organization, consistency of temperament and performance is a must. Leaders must be who they are on a constant basis. They must be steady and stabilizing to the organization. They must always be out in front, performing.

Remember, followers emulate the behavior of the leader. One test of a leader's consistency is the performance of the organization. If it is erratic and unpredictable, that may say something about the leader's consistency, or lack thereof.

Consistency for a leader produces an accumulation of results.

Remember, followers emulate the _____ of the leader.

How can a person help him- or herself become more consistent—in things both great and small?

_____

_____

_____

Is consistency something you need to work on? If so, what are some ideas that can help you improve in this area? Whom can you ask for guidance?

_____

_____

_____

Working: Maintaining Focus

Leadership is largely a game of knowing "what to leave in and what to leave out." For nearly any leader in any position, there will continually be a myriad of attractions and distractions all vying for the leader's attention. True leadership requires the ability to focus. The analogy that comes to mind involves the comparison of a flashlight to a magnifying glass. A flashlight disperses light, while a magnifying glass concentrates it. A leader must be like a magnifying glass, focusing all of his or her efforts upon the main points or priorities. Dispersed, a leader's efforts might not accomplish much more than lighting up a sidewalk; but focused, they can fry insects!

A leader must be like a _____ glass, focusing all of his or her efforts upon the main points or _____.

Do you currently work more like a flashlight or a magnifying glass? How can you increase your focus?

_____

_____

_____

Working: Staying Persistent

Success lies on the other side of inconvenience and struggle. To make it through to the rewards, a leader must learn to persist. How many would-be leaders have failed only because they didn't hang in there long enough? Success in many cases means hanging on after everyone else has been shaken off. Samuel Johnson said, "Great works are performed not by strength but by perseverance."

Leaders recognize that they must hang in there and continue the fight even when all seems lost. Many times, victory is just around the corner.

Success lies on the other side of _____ and

_____.

Many times, _____ is just around the corner.

"Great _____ are performed not by strength but by _____."

Working: Striving Ahead of the Group

Leaders must lead. That means that they must be out front, demonstrating achievement. Leaders must exert a "pull" on their organizations with the strength of their own performance. This is the opposite of "pushing" an organization.

Dwight D. Eisenhower was the commanding general of the Normandy invasion during World War II and the thirty-fourth president of the United States. To explain leadership, Eisenhower was known to reach into his pocket and retrieve a small string. "That piece of string illustrates the main principle of leadership," he would say. "Push the string and you can barely get it to move. But pull the string, and it will follow you anywhere."

Leaders must exert a "_____" on their organizations with the strength of their own performance.

Working: Giving Praise and Recognition

As discussed in the section on motivation, the desire for recognition is universal. Everybody appreciates a sincere compliment.

Leaders look for opportunities to compliment their performers. They specialize in catching people in the act of doing things right, and they don't hesitate to lavish praise.

Leaders look for opportunities to _____ their performers.

Working: Providing Guidance and Course Correction

Ultimately a leader acts as a coach. One definition of a coach is "a vehicle that carries you from where you are to where you want to go." While this definition obviously refers to the horse-and-buggy type of coach, it has cross-application to what a sports or business coach does. An effective leader or coach helps people go places they want to go but are unable to reach on their own. To do this, a leader provides guidance and direction. A leader is courageous in confronting issues that need resolving. When followers are off track, the leader gives correction. Learning how to make these corrections without hurting feelings or dampening enthusiasm is the hallmark of a good leader. This will be explored at length in chapter 9.

Work is the crank that turns the engine in the Cycle of Achievement. A leader must embrace hard work, for all the reasons just discussed. Putting these components together gives the leader productivity toward goals that have been set.

An effective leader or coach helps people go places they want to go but are _____ to reach on their own.

Seeking Counsel

Circle True or False.

True/False   Experience is the best teacher.

Experience is not the best teacher; other people's experience is the best teacher. For this reason, every leader must seek out and find credible mentorship. Without tapping into the experience of others, leaders are forced through a trial-and-error process.

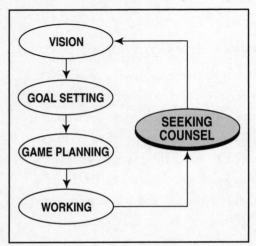

Trial and error is not only painful and frustrating, but it can be extremely time consuming.

Success begins with information from the correct source. Therefore, it is critical that a mentor is chosen based on his or her "fruit on the tree." Receiving mentorship may be done in person with someone interested in sharing his or her wisdom. It may come from studying historical figures with relevance to the undertakings of the leader. Or it may come from studying the materials offered by a speaker or author who can provide wisdom and experience to a leader. By far, the best type of mentor, however, is the personally concerned, face-to-face type. Such a mentor is priceless in the career of a leader.

Later in the workbook, we will delve deeper into the concept of mentoring, as every truly great leader must also become a great mentor. At this stage of our study, we'll focus on the purposes of seeking counsel from a coach or mentor, the case in which the leader is a protégé to another leader (the mentor).

Success begins with _____ from the correct _____.

Do you currently have a mentor? If so, why did you choose that person?

_____
_____
_____

In your opinion, what results or qualities are important for a mentor to have?

_____
_____
_____

A Leader Seeks Counsel to Learn

Seeking counsel from qualified sources is one of the most effective ways for a leader to learn. What can a leader learn from mentorship? A leader can gain information, attitudes, perspectives, judgment, strategies, mind-sets, priorities, and objectives. However, this can never occur without humility on the part of the leader. A leader must humble himself before a mentor and agree to take counsel. Mentors are not there to make leaders feel better or to inflate their egos with unearned praise. Mentors rise above mere friendship and provide needed, straight-ahead guidance. At times, this may be uncomfortable for a developing leader, but the price of discomfort with a mentor is much less than the price of discomfort that comes with mistakes in judgment or poor performance in the field.

Leaders know they always have more to _____.

What are some potential areas you may feel uncomfortable discussing with your mentor?

_____

_____

_____

Would you like to have more success in these areas?

_____

_____

_____

What can you do to feel more comfortable opening up about these areas for help and guidance?

_____

_____

_____

A Leader Seeks Counsel to Gain Perspective

One of the most valuable things to be gained from a mentor is perspective. Webster defines *perspective* as "a view of things in their true relationship or importance." How a leader sees things is paramount. Properly defining a problem, with the correct perspective, is by far the biggest component in finding the solution. Often leaders are simply too close to a situation. They struggle with it and fight it but lose the overall perspective that a mentor can provide. Also, in many cases, mentors have had experience in similar situations and can provide historical perspective.

Perspective: "A _____ of things in their true _____ or _____."

A Leader Seeks Counsel to Make Midcourse Corrections

Even when a leader is clear on the objectives and implements a well-thought-out game plan, things can go awry. Sometimes progress lags behind the plan. When these glitches occur, mentors can provide invaluable insights into changes in the game plan that will still allow for the attainment of the goal.

Picture a person wandering across a great expanse of desert, as shown below:

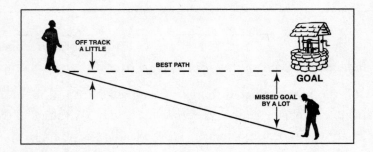

The person's goal is to make it to the well of fresh water several miles in the distance. The wellhead is small and cannot be seen by the traveler, but the traveler knows the general direction in which to walk. Notice how the traveler can get off track just a small amount early in the journey. Notice also how this amplifies throughout the journey to the point where the walker has gone far enough to reach the well, but is still miles away from it. Now let's take a look at another traveler seeking the same fresh water.

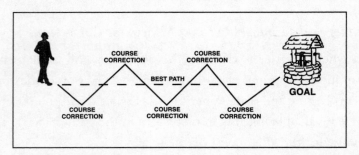

A guide or mentor who has been to the well before accompanies this sojourner. At intervals along the way, the mentor initiates small corrections in direction. At the end of the journey, not only has the mentor saved the traveler a lot of wasted steps, but also has ensured that the traveler makes it to the well and survives to walk another day. And so it is in the life of a leader. Mentors provide these all-important corrections along the way to keep the leader from missing the mark entirely and ending up with disaster.

A Leader Seeks Counsel to Receive Feedback

Just like a student receiving a report card, leaders obtain feedback on their performance from mentors. Leadership can be complicated. In some cases, leaders can become fuzzy-headed regarding their performance. It can be difficult at times to know if progress is being made toward overall objectives. Mentors slice through the confusion and clarify the picture, providing the leader with clear feedback on his or her performance. A mentor can provide a positive outlook, where the leader sees only his own failures. A mentor can also keep the developing leader's head from "swelling" by shining a light on areas for further improvement. This is where it is a big help if goals have been set correctly and game plans are clear and well structured. Mentors can provide feedback on how well the leader is working according to priorities, on the mind-set and attitude of the leader, and on the leader's progress toward the goals.

A Leader Seeks Counsel to Be Held Accountable for Results

How well did the leader do in reaching his objectives? How did the leader grow in understanding and experience? Is the leader progressing in ability and character? The answers to all these questions, while evaluated by the mentor, are the responsibility of the leader. Remember, leadership is a "the buck stops here" profession. Leaders must resist the urge to "candy coat" their performance. Instead, leaders must open up and be entirely honest with their mentors. Only with such a system of accountability can true leadership development be optimized.

Leaders must resist the urge to "_____ _____" their performance.

A Leader Seeks Counsel to Grow Personally

The overall goal of mentorship is to grow the leader. It is fine to advance the leader's performance and help the leader hit some goals, but these are just the playing field on which the athlete is strengthened. The real goal is for the leader to experience significant personal growth. Ultimately, there is no sustainable growth in results without growth in the leader. Leaders must grow personally. It is a fact of life for leaders that they have to get better. And they must commit to growing on a regular basis. As the saying goes, the speed of the leader is the speed of the group. Mentors are there to provide guidance and place a continued emphasis on personal growth.

The speed of the _____ is the speed of the _____.

Why is personal growth so important in leadership?

_____

_____

_____

Have you benefited from mentoring with a leader who helps people with their personal growth? If so, describe the experience.

_____

_____

_____

A Leader Seeks Counsel to Earn Respect

To be respected by the respected is every leader's desire. Said another way, to be blessed by the best overcomes all the rest. Money and fame and power and prestige may all have some charm, but there is nothing like earning the respect of someone who has been instrumental in teaching and guiding our own growth and success. Leaders know this about themselves and strive to earn the respect of their mentors.

To be _____ by the _____ is every leader's desire.

The Cycle of Achievement: Oliver Hazard Perry and the Battle of Lake Erie

The War of 1812, for many, was more properly called the Second War for Independence. The new United States was struggling to make it in the tough world of foreign affairs, and its troubles with England had bubbled up into a war for which the new nation was not ready.

Much of North America was still unsettled, and the "frontier" was the Ohio Valley and the dense forest regions around the Great Lakes. Control of these inland waterways was critical to control of the frontier territory, and both the United States and England were eager to dominate there.

Onto this scene sailed a twenty-seven-year-old American named Oliver Hazard Perry. In a small, freshwater sailing fleet, Perry engaged the bulk of England's Great Lakes squadron in what became the Battle of Lake Erie. Perry commanded the *Lawrence*, a ship named for a recently killed captain of the American navy who had lost one of the United States' six powerful frigates in direct disobedience to orders. Lawrence's reckless conduct had pitched his awesome ship against one of the ablest captains and best-trained crews in the British navy. Lawrence's ship, the *Chesapeake*, was destroyed in less than fifteen minutes! Strangely, Lawrence's dying words, "Don't give up the ship," caught on as a sort of battle cry among the American sailors ever after. Even though Lawrence had foolishly put himself and his crew into a position where giving up their ship was inevitable, the phrase became almost as powerful as "Remember the Alamo" would decades later. Because of this, as Oliver Hazard Perry sailed to confront the British Great Lakes fleet that day, his ship, the *Lawrence*, flew a flag that proudly stated, "Don't Give Up the Ship!"

Although all the ships in the engagement were tiny by ocean-going standards, the Battle of Lake Erie would be the biggest, most violent naval engagement the Great Lakes would ever see. Perry sailed directly into the British ships and fought furiously. The *Lawrence* was one of the two biggest, most powerful American ships on the Great Lakes. The other one was called the *Niagara*. For some reason, though, the *Niagara* didn't engage in the battle. It stood a ways off, out of harm's way, and watched Perry get torn to shreds in the *Lawrence*. Although Perry was fighting a losing battle, he had inflicted heavy casualties on five British ships at once, firing furiously and refusing to quit.

Finally, the *Lawrence* was almost a complete wreck. Four-fifths of Perry's men had been killed or wounded. The gun deck was littered with bodies and refuse, the dead and dying sprawled everywhere. With so much death and destruction, hardly a gun was left firing aboard the *Lawrence*. Still, from the mast of the ship flew the flag that said, "Don't Give Up the Ship!"

At this point in the battle, Perry did the unthinkable. He lowered one of his only remaining ship's boats into the water, and with a small contingent of men, he rowed away from the battle and toward the untouched *Niagara*, which was still watching the battle from a safe distance. Perry and his men in the little boat were fired upon by the same cannon that had torn his ship to pieces.

However, many of the British ships were damaged badly enough that they neither destroyed his boat nor made much of an attempt to pursue. Perhaps they thought the battle was over and Perry was fleeing the scene. But as Perry reached the *Niagara*, he needed only moments to convince the crew to follow his orders instead of those of their timid captain. The *Niagara* made sail and headed directly back to the fleet of damaged British ships.

It is interesting to imagine what the men aboard the British ships must have thought, seeing the heroics of this young captain and his bravery while rowing a boat through heavy enemy fire. How their attitudes must have changed as they realized he was bringing a new ship to engage them! And engage them he did. With the fresh firepower of the *Niagara* brought to bear on the damaged British fleet, the outcome was not even a question. The bravery of Oliver Hazard Perry had won the day and secured the Great Lakes and the western frontier for the United States. Throughout the remainder of the War of 1812, the British would never regain what they had lost that day.

It is interesting to think about Perry's exploits that day in leadership terms. What he did was nearly unprecedented in naval history, but is even more powerful as a metaphor for leadership. The Battle of Lake Erie shows some great illustrations of the Cycle of Achievement.

Perry was able to cast a big enough *vision* and trust in his leadership abilities that he not only managed to keep his crew fighting until the end, but he also convinced an entirely different crew, that of the *Niagara*, to follow his lead. With the *goal* of winning the battle, Perry apparently had a good enough *game plan* and was good at *working* through his plan to last as long as he did in a losing battle in his original ship, the *Lawrence*.

Perry's actions are impressive, especially given the bad advice he had flying from a flag staff aboard his ship. He didn't fall in love with the idea of winning the battle aboard his ship, committing to the chivalrous but silly *counsel* that he should either win or go down with his ship. Instead, with a clear goal in mind, he was willing to disregard the popular naval passions of his time and change his plans in order to achieve victory. Perry demonstrated that day how goals should be set in stone and plans should be set in sand. If the plans aren't working, scrap them and come up with new plans. But never give up the goal! If one ship isn't working, get another ship. But be sure to get to the victory!

Why does the saying "Don't give up the ship" seem so impactful and like the right course of action?

_____

_____

_____

After reading this story, in what ways do you see that the saying "Don't give up the ship" goes against the proper role of a leader?

_____

_____

_____

What other lessons can be learned from this story?

_____

_____

_____

Summary

It is the iterative Cycle of Achievement loop that leaders deploy in their planned attack on the status quo. Understanding each of the parts and using it as a road map allows leaders to improve their performance on a continuing basis. The Cycle of Achievement gives leaders one way to describe that improvement process and keeps them on track as they rotate the cycle over and over again. With every rotation, the leader improves, advances, and betters himself.

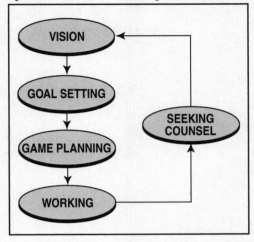

How has learning the Cycle of Achievement increased your ability to grow as a leader?

_____

_____

_____

Out of the five steps of the Cycle of Achievement, which one are you the best at? Why are you better at this step?

_____

_____

_____

Which step needs the most work? What about this step is holding you back the most?

_____

_____

_____

HOW A LEADER GROWS PERSONALLY

CHAPTER 4

The Trilateral Leadership Ledger

*I know of no more encouraging fact than the unquestionable
ability of man to elevate his life by conscious endeavor.*
—HENRY DAVID THOREAU

Hugo Grotius was a Dutch lawyer, writer, theologian, and statesman in the late sixteenth and early seventeenth centuries. President
James Madison called him the "father of the modern code of nations." On the topic of self-government, Grotius boiled the idea
of leadership all the way down to the level of the individual. He
said, "He knows not how to rule a Kingdom, that cannot manage
a Province; nor can he wield a Province, that cannot order a City;
nor he order a City, that knows not how to regulate a Village; nor
he a Village, that cannot guide a Family; nor can that man Govern
well a Family that knows not how to Govern himself." Authors
Mark Beliles and Stephen McDowell simplified it even further:
"You must rule yourself before you rule others." Too often in our
world we see individuals attempting to influence others when they
are barely able to lead themselves. To become a leader, one must

gain self-mastery, which can be accomplished only through a pro-gram of deliberate personal growth.

"You must rule _____ before you rule _____."

For leaders, growth cannot be optional. The only way to keep pace with increasing responsibilities is through increased ability. Growth, then, must occur in two categories:

1. Personal
2. Influence with others

For leaders, _____ cannot be optional.

This chapter focuses on the first of these, the personal-growth side of leadership development, while the next six chapters will tackle the subject of influence. Personal growth is first because a leader's ability to influence others stems from his or her personal abilities.

Personal growth is *internal*, taking place deep within a leader. Often, when people embark upon the journey of becoming lead-ers, they feel frustrated at a lack of external results to show for their efforts. But the process of becoming a leader starts with a lot of effort, which results in improvements the outside world cannot yet see. The gains are internal, inside the person. Only later will all the effort at personal growth and improvement show up in the form of external results. Stephen Covey said, "Internal victories precede external victories."

Because personal growth is internal and the external results show up only much later, we have found it helpful to give leaders a way to self-assess their effectiveness and track their progress. We do this using what we call a Trilateral Leadership Ledger, shown below.

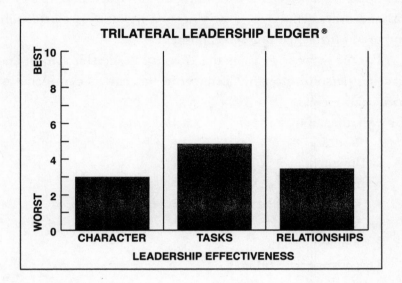

On the left vertical scale of this chart is the ranking of the effectiveness of the leader, with 10 being perfect and 0 being dismal. Across the bottom horizontal scale are the categories of leadership effectiveness. It should be the goal of a leader to grow in the mastery of each of these three areas.

The Three Categories of Personal Effectiveness

Character

We discussed character and the concept of honor in "What a Leader Brings," but it bears further discussion here. We can't emphasize this too much: Nobody lacking character will succeed in a meaningful way.

One of the first things a person on the leadership-development journey should understand is that there is intrinsic value in developing character even if he never obtains external results from his endeavors. This is because who one becomes is much more important than what one accomplishes.

For the purpose of using the Trilateral Leadership Ledger and gauging personal growth, Character in this case is considered to include:

1. honesty
2. integrity
3. courage
4. proper values based on absolute truths
5. faith
6. a humble spirit
7. patience with others
8. discipline
9. self-mastery

Nobody lacking _____ will succeed in a meaningful way.

Tasks

The Tasks category simply represents the ability to get things done. It comprehends all the concepts of "Work" we discussed in the Cycle of Achievement. No leader can succeed without the ability to execute tasks. For assessing a leader's effectiveness and monitoring growth, the Tasks category includes:

1. acceptance of responsibility
2. work ethic

3. availability
4. willingness to invest time
5. tenacity
6. perseverance
7. execution

No leader can succeed without the ability to execute
_____.

Relationships

The category of Relationships measures the ability to get along with and form lasting bonds with people. No leader can experience success alone. Such a situation precludes the very concept of leadership. Leaders must accomplish things through, with, and for people, and that can happen only with the ability to build relationships. The Relationships category includes:

1. accepting people
2. approving of people
3. appreciating people
4. seeing the good in people
5. encouraging people
6. caring for and about people
7. putting others first
8. seeking win-win arrangements
9. helping people accomplish tasks
10. living the "Golden Rule"

Leaders must accomplish things through, with, and for
_____.

Using the Trilateral Leadership Ledger

A leader can begin the personal-growth journey with a self-assessed rating on the Ledger. That will provide a starting point. As the leader progresses using the principles taught in this workbook, there will be marked improvements, which can then be estimated using the chart. In this way, a leader can keep him- or herself on track and make sure there is not only growth, but growth in all three categories.

Here's how it works. Let's say a certain leader, Mister A., has a fairly high starting score for Character. He estimates himself to be a 4. Next, he knows he is not very task-oriented and is prone to procrastination and making excuses, so he rates himself a 1 in the Tasks category. Finally, Mister A. thinks he is decent at building and sustaining relationships and gives himself a 3 in Relationships. Multiplying the three together gives him a total score of 12. Mister A. uses that as his starting score of Leadership Effectiveness.

One note of caution: In general, people tend to overrate themselves. Often the gap between self-realization and reality is enormous.

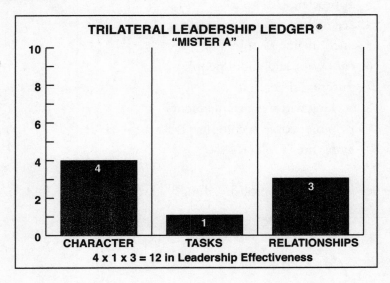

The best use of the Leadership Ledger for someone on the leadership-development journey is to make an honest assessment of his or her starting point. Jim Collins calls it "confronting brutal reality." Asking a mentor's opinion on this self-evaluation may make it more realistic. Only when leaders are courageous enough to face the facts as they really are can they properly size up the challenge and respond appropriately. Leaders can improve only when they decide to improve. And they cannot improve unless they know where they are weak and where they are strong. We don't control where we start our journeys, but we *do* control what we do once we've started. The goal is to take what we've been given and do the most we can with it.

Let's get a basic idea of what your current score of Leadership Effectiveness might be. Rate yourself from 0 to 10 (0 being the lowest and 10 being perfect) in the areas of Character, Tasks, and Relationships.

Character

_____ 1. honesty

_____ 2. integrity

_____ 3. courage

_____ 4. proper values based on absolute truths

_____ 5. faith

_____ 6. a humble spirit

_____ 7. patience with others

_____ 8. discipline

_____ 9. self-mastery

Total score = _____ ÷ 9 = _____ average score

Which were your two lowest scores? How can you work on improving those scores?

_____

_____

_____

Which were your two highest scores? Why are these higher than the rest?

_____

_____

Tasks

_____ 1. acceptance of responsibility

_____ 2. work ethic

_____ 3. availability

_____ 4. willingness to invest time

_____ 5. tenacity

_____ 6. perseverance

_____ 7. execution

Total score = _____ ÷ 7 = _____ average score

Which were your two lowest scores? How can you work on improving those scores?

_____

_____

Which were your two highest scores? Why are these higher than the rest?

_____

Relationships

_____ 1. accepting people
_____ 2. approving of people
_____ 3. appreciating people
_____ 4. seeing the good in people
_____ 5. encouraging people
_____ 6. caring for and about people
_____ 7. putting others first
_____ 8. seeking win-win arrangements
_____ 9. helping people accomplish tasks
_____ 10. living the "Golden Rule"

Total score = _____ ÷ 10 = _____ average score

Which were your two lowest scores? How can you work on improving those scores?

_____

_____

Which were your two highest scores? Why are these higher than the rest?

_____

_____

To better evaluate yourself, talk to someone whom you trust, preferably your mentor, and ask if he or she will honestly score you as well. Now, your mentor's score of you might differ in range, but you can get an idea of your observed strengths and weaknesses.

Fill in the following Leadership Ledger with your total scores.

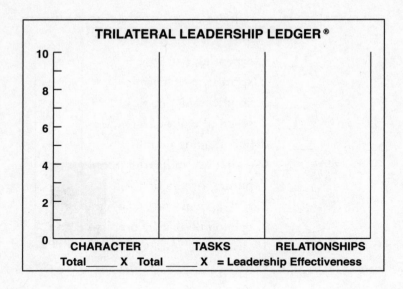

A newer leader will most likely be fairly weak in all categories. Multiplying the numbers will not result in much of a score. Also, the poorer a leader is in the beginning, the smaller the numbers in each category. That means more effort is required to make an impact on the overall score. For instance, let's say Mister A. improves his ability to build relationships from a 3, where he started, to a 4. Recalculating his total score would give him a Leadership Effectiveness of 16, as compared to 12 when he began.

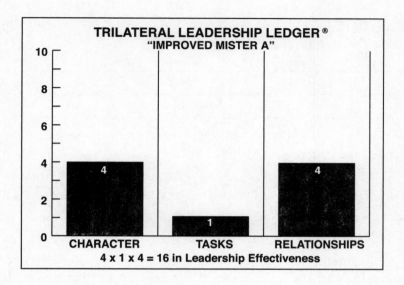

When you consider that perfect Leadership Effectiveness would have a score of 1,000 (10 x 10 x 10), moving from a 12 to a 16 is not very significant. This is why we say that budding leaders need patience and perseverance. It will take time and effort to improve to the point where external differences can be seen. But by using the Leadership Ledger as a yardstick, Mister A. has moved from a 12 to a 16, which is a 33 percent improvement in his overall Leadership Effectiveness! On a relative basis, that is a huge improvement. The outside world may not be able to tell it yet, but Mister A. is on his way.

Why would it be wrong for those on the outside to prejudge Mister A.'s growth at this point?

_____

_____

_____

If people in the outside world see him working really hard, why might they not be able to see any results?

_____

_____

_____

Circle True or False.

True/False   Focus on your strengths, and your weaknesses will take care of themselves.

We have heard it said that one should focus on his or her strengths, and the weaknesses will take care of themselves. In the more lopsided cases, the Leadership Ledger shows this to be false. Let's consider the person who generates decent scores in two categories but a really low one in the remaining category. Mister B. assesses himself with a Character rating of 3, a Tasks rating of 6, and a Relationships rating of 0. Multiplying the numbers, we can see that no matter how much character Mister B. develops or how many tasks Mister B. accomplishes, he is doomed to have no Leadership Effectiveness because his Relationship score is so abysmal, meaning that he is not good at maintaining relationships. Anything times zero is still zero.

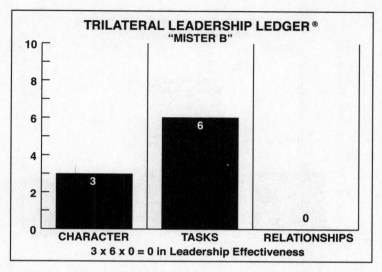

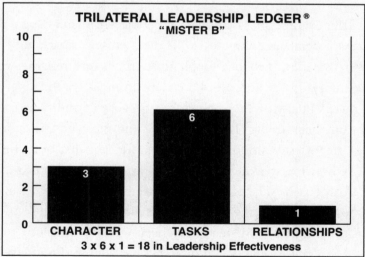

What if Mister B. increases his Relationships score to a 1? His overall Leadership Effectiveness score would still be only 18 out of a possible 1,000.

What if Mister B. improved his strongest area, Tasks, from 6 to 8? That would be an incredible improvement. An assessment of 8 is really getting up there, but yet it would result in a score of just 24!

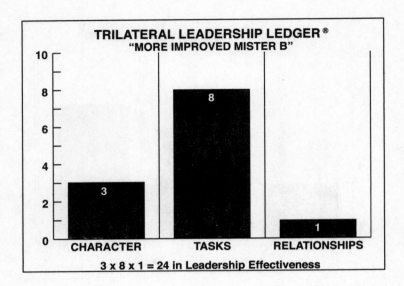

In this example, it is obvious that people like Mister B. who have an area of significant weakness will hold themselves back until they grow in that area. It is not enough just to focus on strengths; weaknesses must also be addressed. Leaders do not have the luxury of being weak in any of these categories because of the catastrophic effect on their results. To be a leader, one must be strong in all three categories—period. It will take work, but that must be the goal. Otherwise, weaknesses will undo strengths. As famed Duke basketball coach Mike Krzyzewski once noted, "Never let a person's weakness get in the way of his strength."

A third example: Mister C. has been working diligently to become a leader for quite some time. He has followed the development process outlined in this workbook and has made conscious decisions to improve in all three areas on the Ledger. Last year, Mister C. rated himself a 6 for Character, a 6 for Tasks, and a 7 for Relationships. His score was 6 times 6 times 7, for a total of 252.

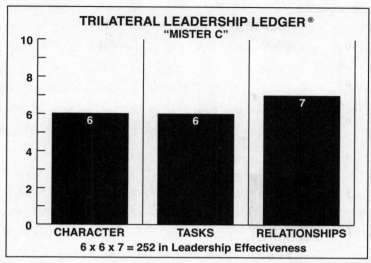

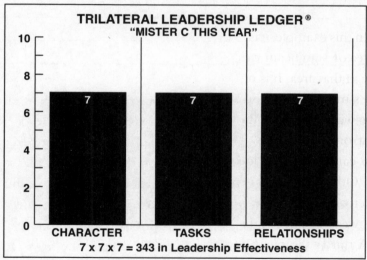

Working hard in all three categories, Mister C. raised himself by just one point in both Character and Tasks, but didn't feel he improved his ability any in the Relationships area. His score now consists of 7 times 7 times 7, for a total leadership effectiveness of 343!

Mister C. raised his score 91 points, or 36 percent, and he improved by merely 1 point in two categories. What Mister C. is experiencing is the compounding effect of accumulated effort. Leadership has a compounding effect. It is the exponential return on effort obtained by a group of people aligned in common purpose that accomplish more than the sum of the whole.

This compounding effect is the very reason leaders influence other people. The Trilateral Leadership Ledger is a way that demonstrates and tracks a leader's improvement and scope of influence.

It could be so easy to quit when Mister A. works really hard to take his Relationships category up 1 point, but increases his total effectiveness by only 2 points. Why would this be the wrong time to quit? Why should he stay the course and raise another category by a small increment?

_____

_____

_____

Many people become curious about their own ranking using the Trilateral Leadership Ledger. As we stated before, a leader will most likely be fairly weak in all categories in the beginning. In fact, most people evaluating themselves for the first time will score much closer to 0 in each category than they will to 10. Additionally, many would-be leaders have zero overall influence because they are zeroed out in one of the categories. Think of the character issues of the leaders of Enron and Tyco and the high-profile corporate scandals of recent years. No matter how inspirational those leaders' leadership styles were, they have no long-term influence because of character problems. A deficiency of the same magnitude in either the Tasks or Relationships category will keep a leader from moving off of 0 as well.

Perhaps some specific estimates will be illustrative. We have found that an individual with a total score of 50 to 100 points is capable of leading smaller groups of people. Such a leader has the character to be followed, a solid work ethic, and an ability to get along with others. Moving upward to a total score of 200 to 300 puts one in rarer company. At this level one is capable of leading large groups of people (notice we didn't say *managing*) and has a near impeccable character score, a work ethic that inspires others, and an ability to create vision and mold a group into a solid team. A person with a score above 300 is a leader sought after by corporations and volunteer groups as a known influencer of people on a large scale. Very few will ever attain this level, but it is available to everyone willing to develop the art and science of leadership.

As leaders, and human ones at that, we will never arrive at perfection. The score of 1,000 is unattainable, but we should never cease in our pursuit of it, closing the gap between where we are and perfection on a regular basis. If we think we have arrived at "good enough," even for a moment, our progress will stop. Worse, it may even go backward. Too many stories can be told of great leaders rising to tremendous influence only to regress rapidly because of reversals in character, effort, or concern for others.

Now that you have read more and have a better understanding of the Trilateral Leadership Ledger, go back to redo your personal rankings. Did they change? If so, why?

_____

_____

_____

Personal Growth: Benjamin Franklin
"Arriving at Moral Perfection"

Benjamin Franklin was one of the United States' most distinguished and diverse founding fathers. He lived a long and prosperous life, lived a "rags to riches" story, spoke several languages, dined with ambassadors and philosophers, was published in many countries, enjoyed worldwide fame, and was one of the only signers of both the Declaration of Independence and the Constitution of the United States (and he also signed the Treaty of Paris, which ended the Revolutionary War). Franklin was the key architect of the alliance between the young United States of America and the world's second superpower, France, and in so doing, he established the means of winning the war with England. He was the creator and writer of *Poor Richard's Almanac*, one of the most widely read annual publications in the New World. He invented bifocals, the enormously popular Franklin stove, and even a musical instrument for which Mozart composed a specific piece of music. His experiments in electricity thrilled the world and initiated the age of electrical discovery and application. He founded the American Philosophical Society, was instrumental in the birth of the University of Pennsylvania, established the first library in the colonies, and worked to organize the early fire departments in Philadelphia.

Franklin's life may best be considered in three distinct phases. First was his early life as a printer, writer, and businessman. In these years, he learned to become a "gentleman" (even though he was not of "proper" birth, a major factor in his day) and amassed a fortune that would support him the rest of his life and outlive him by two centuries. The second phase was his time spent as a "natural philosopher" or scientist and inventor. It was during these years that his fame increased to international proportions, culminating in his membership and active participation in the English Philosophical Society. Finally, his later life was spent as a statesman, representing some of the British colonies on the North American coast and ultimately the fledgling United States of America.

How did he accomplish so much in just one lifetime? How did he rise so high to end up wielding such power and command so much respect around the world? The answers could fill volumes of books. The obvious, though, is that he was a genius. But even geniuses must follow the laws of success, and, besides, Benjamin Franklin's remarkable achievements were the result of his deliberate efforts. He was not lucky. He did not "back into" his accomplishments. He worked hard and tirelessly throughout his life.

There is a story Franklin himself tells in his autobiography about his troubles with relating to people as a young man. A confidant took him aside one day and was both bold and kind enough to share the truth with Franklin that people didn't like him. Although he was amazingly brilliant, nobody cared. They couldn't stand to be around him. He was too argumentative and opinionated. His informer even told him that people would see Franklin approaching on the street and cross the road so as to avoid any contact with him. Franklin was devastated. But his reaction to the cold, hard truth was perhaps one of the most important components in his meteoric success. As a young man, he decided to do something about it.

First, Franklin began tempering his statements to people so as not to offend. He worked hard to become less dogmatic in his choices of words and tones of voice. Then, a few years later, while sailing from England back to the colonies, he undertook "the bold and arduous Project of arriving at moral Perfection," commenting that "I was surprised to find myself so much fuller of faults than I had imagined." So Benjamin Franklin did what we've been discussing in this chapter: he deliberately set out upon a program of personal growth. He selected thirteen virtues he felt worthy of his attention and organized a demanding schedule of improvement and tracking. He would work on one virtue for four weeks at a time, recording his progress or lack thereof, and then move on to the next virtue, repeating the cycle over and over throughout several years. Regarding his faults that had surprised him so much, he "had the satisfaction of seeing them diminish." As an old man he would say about his little project, "But on the whole, though I never arrived at the Perfection I had been so ambitious of obtain-

ing, but fell far short of it, yet I was by the Endeavor made a better
and a happier man than I otherwise should have been, if I had not
attempted it; as those who aim at perfect writing by imitating the
engraved copies, though they never reach the wished for excellence
of those copies, their hand is mended by the endeavor, and is toler-
able while it continues fair and legible."

Franklin's thirteen virtues were as follows. We have labeled
them according to how they fit into the three categories repre-
sented on the Trilateral Leadership Ledger.

1. Temperance (Character)
2. Silence (Character, Relationships)
3. Order (Tasks)
4. Resolution (Tasks)
5. Frugality (Character, Tasks)
6. Industry (Tasks)
7. Sincerity (Character, Relationships)
8. Justice (Character, Relationships)
9. Moderation (Character)
10. Cleanliness (Character, Tasks)
11. Tranquility (Character)
12. Chastity (Character)
13. Humility (Character, Relationships)

Just as we have described the journey of personal growth for a
leader involving self-assessment, willful change, and measurement
of progress, Ben Franklin and his thirteen virtues followed the
same principles.

With a reminder that improvement and growth is a self-guided
mission, Franklin said, "We may give advice, but we cannot give
conduct." Each leader must take it upon him- or herself to grow
personally, just as Benjamin Franklin did. And if it was a worthy

endeavor for a man of such genius, what may its worth be to the less endowed?

How did Benjamin Franklin benefit from the principles of the Trilateral Leadership Ledger?

_____

_____

_____

Where would Franklin be if he had given up and not continued to consistently grow in these areas over a long period of time?

_____

_____

_____

Where would the United States be if he had not confronted the truth and decided to grow personally?

_____

_____

_____

What else can we learn from Benjamin Franklin's story?

_____

_____

_____

Summary

Personal growth is not an option for a leader. The Bible says we will never be given more than we can handle. Therefore, if we want more, we must develop the capacity to handle more. The Trilateral

Leadership Ledger is both a tool for instruction on the great principles of self-improvement and a tracking device for actual application. As leaders understand that their conduct is up to them and the amplification of their natural gifts is their responsibility, they will have set out upon the path of personal growth and increased effectiveness. As they take charge of improving personally, leaders can next begin embracing the idea of increasing their influence with others.

Describe a situation when you were part of a team that was led by a person who was placed in charge because of his knowledge or position, but not his leadership abilities.

_____

_____

_____

_____

_____

_____

HOW A LEADER GROWS IN INFLUENCE

CHAPTER 5

The Five Levels of Influence

A true leader inspires others to lead themselves.
—ARI D. KAPLAN

Progressive Leadership is about the increasing ability of a leader to expand his or her *influence*. As a leader grows in ability, the leader's influence grows as well, but this is not an automatic process. If a leader is to maximize his potential and his influence, the process must be deliberate. Expanding the influence of a leader is accomplished by growing the leader himself.

The Five Levels of Influence are a convenient way to map the journey of a leader from beginning to crowning achievement. The leader grows in stature and ability to influence by ascending these steps. Each level presents more influence and takes greater advantage of the abilities of the leader by amplifying those abilities across a broader spectrum.

If a leader is to maximize his _____ and his _____, the process must be _____.

Expanding the _____ of a leader is accomplished by growing the leader himself.

Levels of Leadership

The concept of various levels of leadership (and hence, influence) is found in several sources, but two stand out above the others.

The first is from renowned leadership expert John C. Maxwell in his book *Developing the Leader within You*. Maxwell also suggests that there are Five Levels of Leadership, given here in ascending power of influence:

1. Position
2. Permission
3. Production
4. People Development
5. Personhood

Maxwell explains that Level 1, Position, is leadership based upon title alone. There is no credibility for this leader except for his official authority. Next is Permission, where a leader is allowed to lead because his followers allow it. Production is when followers pursue a leader because the leader gets results. People Development is when people like and respect the leader and experience an increased performance when dealing with that leader. Personhood is the rare condition when a leader has established a large following and achieved massive results based on his character and longevity. These levels help to make sense of the myriad of leadership ability encountered on a daily basis.

The second source for this idea of Levels of Leadership is Jim Collins, author of *Good to Great*. In that best-selling book, Collins presents the following Five Levels of Leadership, again in ascending order of effectiveness:

1. Capable Individual
2. Contributing Team Member
3. Competent Orchestrator
4. Effective Leader
5. Executive

Collins says a Capable Individual (Level 1) is someone who has obtained core competencies and basic abilities. A Contributing Team Member functions well as part of a group effort. A Competent Orchestrator is skilled at coordinating the efforts of Contributing Team Members. An Effective Leader is one with a broader vision and the ability to direct the Orchestrators toward big-picture objectives. And the highest elevation in Collins's hierarchy of leadership is the Executive, with whom full directional responsibility for the organization resides.

These experts on leadership have given us an enormous insight into clarifying a difficult subject. Mapping the path of a leader to greatness is no easy challenge, especially when the goal of that map is to provide a straightforward route for up-and-coming leaders. Maxwell and Collins have surveyed the wild country. It is the intention of this book to settle that territory into smaller, usable plots. Building upon their ideas and examining them at a pragmatic level will provide the developing leader with increased clarity on the leadership-development process.

Why would it be important to classify levels of leadership?

_____

_____

_____

Have you heard of other ways of describing levels of leadership? If so, how similar are they?

_____

_____

_____

The Five Levels of Influence Explained

This concept of Levels of Influence will be explored within the framework of the following hierarchy:

1. Learning
2. Performing
3. Leading
4. Developing Leaders
5. Developing Developers of Leaders

As with Maxwell and Collins, these Five Levels are in ascending order, but they are slightly different from those of either author.

A previous diagram may be helpful here. Earlier we discussed the Foundational Qualities a leader must possess to gain entrance through the door and onto the playing field of leadership. Next were the Cycle of Achievement and personal growth. Now it is time to explore the playing field of leadership.

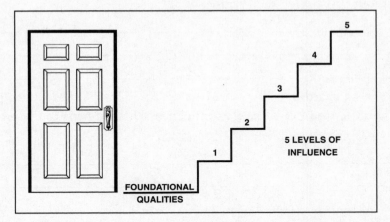

Note that the playing field is not level. It is more like a flight of ascending stairs. This is because as a leader progresses through the leadership-development process, his influence increases and the impact of his efforts has broader scope. Also, as the leader ascends the Levels of Influence, each of the previous levels stays with him. Just because a leader has advanced to the level of Performing doesn't mean he stops Learning. Likewise, a leader who advances to Developing Leaders cannot stop Leading in other areas, and so on.

So the Five Levels of Influence represent a progressive process where a leader picks up new abilities while accumulating and expanding his or her influence. A leader may be at various Levels of Influence in different areas of his or her life. Also, organizations themselves can exist at different levels on this progression. Finally, individuals within the organization each exist at their own Level of Influence. These realizations are helpful in pinpointing where individuals and organizations are and for developing plans for growth and improvement.

Why can't someone start progressing up the Levels of Influence without first having the Foundational Qualities?

_____

_____

_____

When you move up a Level in Influence, what happens to the previous Levels of Influence?

_____

_____

_____

With this brief explanation, where do you see yourself on the Levels of Influence? As you read on, hopefully you'll be able to get a better understanding of what level you are on.

_____

_____

_____

Having learned the Levels of Influence, what would you like to do with that understanding?

_____

_____

_____

Living the Five Levels of Influence: Queen Elizabeth I

Perhaps one of the best examples of a leader ascending through various levels of leadership is England's Queen Elizabeth I. Born in the tumultuous sixteenth century to the infamous King Henry VIII, Elizabeth proved her mettle at first by simply surviving. Her father had her mother executed, and Elizabeth was later framed in a complicated power struggle within the English royal court. This kept her under suspicion and confinement during the entire reign of her cousin Edward VI. Then later, when her half-sister Mary I (later to be called Bloody Mary) gained control of the English throne, Elizabeth was in constant danger of being killed by order of the jealous and religiously opposite queen. Elizabeth did not waste her time in confinement, however, but used it wisely by taking all the advantage she could of the education available to royalty.

Elizabeth's period of learning and survival finally gave birth to her chance to perform, as she attained the throne upon the death of Mary. As she became queen, Elizabeth faced a country on the brink of civil war, and, worse, she gained power in a time and place where women were not thought fit to rule. The privations of her sister before her didn't help matters, either. But Elizabeth's leadership ability was immediately apparent. According to author Alan Axelrod in *Profiles in Leadership*, "She quickly established a charismatic rapport with the crowds....Elizabeth made it clear that she meant to return England...to greatness in trade and among the nations."

Elizabeth's next level of leadership was evidenced by her acute ability to surround herself with loyal talent. Axelrod states, "Celebrated for her strong will, Elizabeth nevertheless gathered about herself the best and brightest political and economic minds of England to serve as her advisers." This ever-increasing ring of power would eventually include such notables as Sir Francis Drake, John Hawkins, and Sir Walter Raleigh, who, as seafaring adventurers, would be instrumental in defeating the mighty Spanish Armada (with some help from the weather). In the course of her reign, Elizabeth had taken a chaotic and quarrelsome, economically tiny country and put it on the path to becoming the most prosperous in Europe.

At her highest level of leadership influence, Elizabeth created a stable political climate and tradition that endured even after her death. It was during her reign of over four decades that English people developed a strong national pride and sense of "country-hood." This was to carry down through generations. As much as any leader, Queen Elizabeth I demonstrates with her life the results that are possible through the ascending Levels of Influence available to a leader.

What time in Elizabeth's life was spent at the Leadership Level 1? Level 2? Level 3? Level 4?

_____

_____

_____

Can you recognize the ascending Levels of Leadership from other figures of history?

_____

_____

_____

Summary

Exploration of the Five Levels of Influence in the following chapters demonstrates that leadership is both an art (requiring thinking) and a science (requiring action). Arguments have raged for centuries as to whether leadership is an art, that is, based upon talent and largely "discerned" by the capable, or whether it is a science, meaning that it's simply skill-based and can be "learned" by anyone. The upcoming pages contend that leadership is fairly considered to be *both* art and science.

For each of the Five Levels of Influence, there are presuppositions, or mind-sets, that are required for a leader to perform at that Level. This is the "art" portion of leadership. Yet each Level is not complete without actions, or the "science" side. The presuppositions will be discussed first because understanding the thinking behind actions always results in more effective actions.

The next several chapters assist developing leaders in discerning and understanding the thinking or "art" involved in leadership, while learning and applying the actions or "science" side.

CHAPTER 6

The First Level of Influence: Learning

That is one of the great secrets of becoming a great leader—never stop becoming.

—JEFF O'LEARY

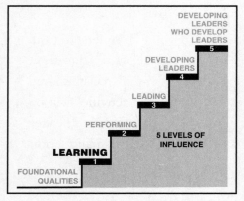

The first of the Levels of Influence is becoming a student. Being hone-able and learning from others have already been stated as keys to leadership success, but here the concept is analyzed at greater depth.

At this First Level of Influence, a leader is a little like a child running onto the field for her first soccer game. She is full of hunger and enthusiasm, but has a low level of skill and knows very little about the sport. It is not time to worry too much about winning. It is not time to be overly concerned with appearances or making impressions on the coach. It is time to *learn*.

Leaders must fall in love with learning. They must resist the temptation to be judgmental or critical or block out the fact that they have something to learn. Every great leader realizes that he still has more to discover. Author Andy Stanley observed, "Great leaders are great learners."

Leaders must fall in love with _____.

"Great leaders are great _____."

Do you love to learn? Do you already have a habit of a self-directed education? If not, what are some areas you look forward to learning about and progressing in?

_____

_____

_____

Presuppositions or the "Art" of Learning

When it comes to Level 1, would-be leaders must understand the foundational thought processes that open the doors to education. We call these presuppositions. Without a base of correct thinking, learning will be difficult, and the proper learning activities will be resisted, missed, or at least not fully utilized. But when a leader understands the very concept of learning and the mentality upon which it is based, education can truly occur.

Learning Is a Top Priority

Initial and ongoing education is crucial for a leader. This education is not necessarily formal or "credentialed." Learning for a leader can occur in many ways. The key is that learning becomes a staple food in the mental diet of the leader. At Level 1, leaders must realize that they are only as good as what they learn and apply.

This education is not necessarily _____ or "_____."

Leaders Can Learn from Anyone

Leaders must be aware that opportunities for learning are all around them. Education, information, insight, and wisdom can come from any source. Nobody is "below" the leader. Something can be learned from anyone. As Dale Carnegie wrote, "Everyone is your superior in some way."

"Everyone is your _____ in some way."

Leaders Can Learn Best from Those Who Have Results

Although it is true that something can be learned from anybody, it is equally true *that the best education comes from those who have results in life*, in particular, those who have success in the exact area of concern where the leader operates. Doesn't it make sense to learn about becoming a physician from a successful doctor? Wouldn't the information about starting a business be most valuable from a successful entrepreneur? As the saying goes, "Success begins with information from the correct source."

The best education comes from those who have _____ in life.

"Success begins with _____ from the _____ _____."

Actions or the "Science" of Learning

Standing firmly on the aforementioned presuppositions, the student can then focus on the actions or science side of learning. These can be considered the *skills* of learning, or what a leader learns about.

Leaders Learn about People

Leaders know that people are what leadership is all about, and they understand that it is only through people that leaders have influence. It is *with*, *through*, and *for* people that leadership exists.

Perhaps you've heard the cliché that "an organization's most important resource is its people." The statement should actually be refined to say, "An organization's best resource is the *right* people," for the right people are the heart of progress, while the wrong people are just the opposite (and everybody knows that the opposite of "pro-gress" is "con-gress"). Therefore, leaders must become experts at dealing with people and determining who the *right* people are to hire, recruit, train, and develop. This is true in both a general and a specific sense.

First of all, leaders must be well disciplined in the art of human relations, and this cannot be only at a superficial, surface level. There is nothing worse than a would-be leader pumped full of people skills but operating from a devious heart. People don't care how much a leader knows until they know *how much he cares*. If the leader has character and his heart is right, people will trust and follow him. Then and only then do people *skills* come into play, and these skills are very important.

Second, a leader must learn about his people *specifically*. Great leaders take an active, sincere interest in other people. One of the most effective ways for leaders to learn about each of their people is to find something in common with them. Picture a boat circling an island, looking for a port at which to dock. A connection is made when the boat makes landfall and snuggles safely into the harbor. Leaders must connect with their people in a similar fashion, taking the time to circle and discover a point of commonality where contact can be made and a relationship can be initiated.

Learning how to deal with people in a general sense and learning *about* them in a specific and caring way are ongoing processes for any leader.

It is *with*, *through*, and *for* _____ that leadership exists.

People don't care how much a leader _____ until they know how much he _____.

Great leaders take an active, sincere interest in other _____.

Why is learning about people so important in leadership?

_____

_____

_____

Since people don't care how much a leader knows until they know how much he cares, what are some ways you can show people that you care about them?

_____

_____

_____

Leaders Learn about Basics

Everything a leader knows at the top she learns at the bottom. This is the part of the leadership-development process where the leader gains an intricate knowledge of the fundamentals in her field. Learning the basics is not optional. Under no circumstances can a successful leader skip this step. As the leader begins to perform and make mistakes, she falls forward, gets up, and tries again. It is in this "productive loop" where the leader becomes strong and capable.

Everything a leader knows at the _____ she learns at the _____.

What are some of the basics in your field?

_____

_____

_____

Leaders Learn about Goals and Objectives

Leaders must learn all they can about the goals and objectives that are required or expected of their organization. An organization cannot hit a target that doesn't exist, and it is a leader's job to learn all there is to learn about the group's requirements. This is doubly important because it also falls to the leader to articulate a vision to the organization of achieving the goals that are before them.

An organization cannot hit a _____ that doesn't exist.

Leaders Learn about Processes

Understanding the processes involved in their areas is a necessity for leaders. It will be the responsibility of the leader to evaluate these processes and perhaps make adjustments and improvements, but this will be premature if the leader has not worked to master the processes. Learning all there is to know about the processes will also give the leader credibility when dealing with subordinates who may be closer to and more involved with the daily details.

Then, leaders can work with the people in the organization either to make improvements in the processes or to ensure that the existing processes are executed properly.

Leaders Learn about Measurements of Performance

Leaders must thoroughly learn the metrics used to determine performance levels in their organization. This is true in a large, overall sense and also at the detail level for each of the people in the leader's sphere of influence. Leaders cannot operate solely on "feel." There must be concrete measurements of performance that provide the leader with ongoing feedback.

Leaders cannot operate solely on "_____."

Leaders Learn about Rewards

No leader can lead without a solid understanding of the rewards of performance in his field. This is true for himself personally and for the people in his organization. This is because motivation is critical to properly casting a vision and maximizing performance. A leader who neglects to learn all there is to learn in this critical category leaves a valuable weapon in the holster.

Leaders Learn about Histories

"Those who cannot remember the past are condemned to repeat it," said philosopher George Santayana. Leaders must take an active interest in the history of their organization. There are valuable lessons to be learned that can save time and energy. Not knowing the lessons of the past also compromises the leader's credibility with his people, who may have actually lived through some of the events.

A big part of learning the history of an organization is learning about its successes. Who has made it big? How did they do it?

Why did they experience success? Are they available for firsthand instruction? What processes seemed to work the best? What innovations were implemented? What could have been done to bring an even bigger impact? What were the pitfalls that were avoided? Asking these types of questions and studying up on the successes of the past are an allowable shortcut every leader should pursue.

It has been said that we learn more from our failures than we ever do from our successes. *Failure that teaches a lesson is simply tuition toward a future success.* As leaders endeavor to lead, they will make mistakes and experience failures. Astute leaders know to extract every ounce of lesson from each mistake, understanding that the lesson continues until the lesson is learned. Great leaders are not those who never make mistakes. Great leaders are those who learn quickly and most effectively from their mistakes.

Failure that teaches a _____ is simply tuition toward a future _____.

Leaders Learn about Environment

In *Authentic Leadership*, Bill George writes, "The leader's job is to provide an empowering environment." Leaders must learn about the environment in their organizations and use that knowledge to enhance and maximize it. People need an empowering, exciting, positive, encouraging environment where mistakes are accepted as long as they are learned from, where success is rewarded, and where processes make sense and get results. The archway over all of this is the leader's own attitude and outlook. This, more than anything else, sets the tone for the organization and creates the right environment. Smart leaders never stop learning about their organization's environment and ways to enhance it.

The archway over all of this is the leader's own _____
and _____.

Leaders Learn about Obstacles and Oppositions

Roadblocks are scattered all along the highway of success. Leaders are wise to be diligent and knowledgeable about these pitfalls. Learning about obstructions in the path to achievement and properly defining them is a necessary part of continual learning.

Many leaders tend to continue hammering away at the same old challenges without ever stopping to see if they are having an effect. Einstein wrote, "Insanity: doing the same thing over and over again and expecting different results." Remember, properly defining a problem is the biggest part of solving it. Learning about obstacles and challenges to an organization also gives the leader information to share with mentors in seeking ways to resolve them.

Along with obstacles comes opposition. It seems that no matter what a leader's undertaking, there will always be someone opposed to it. Learning all that can be done to neutralize those in opposition to a leader's goals can be crucial to the organization's success. Often, though, simply ignoring those in opposition is the best course of action. Usually, the best antidote for criticism is success. Learning that principle may be one of a leader's most important lessons.

"Insanity: doing the same thing over and over again and expecting _____ _____."

Usually, the best antidote for criticism is _____.

When he or she understands these *areas* of learning, or what a leader learns about, a leader should then take full advantage of all *methods* of learning available, or the sources from which a leader learns.

Leaders Learn from Books

Harry Truman said, "Not all readers are leaders, but all leaders must be readers." It is a fact that most of the greatest leaders throughout history have been avid readers. As a young boy, Napoleon read books constantly. Thomas Jefferson bought books compulsively throughout his life and read them with even more vigor than he collected them. Singer and songwriter Jimmy Buffett said of his mother, "She taught me that reading is the key to everything."

Books represent the accumulated knowledge and wisdom of the ages, available for pennies on the dollar. Books preserve the greatest thoughts, the greatest ideas, and the greatest insights of human experience. Roy L. Smith said, "A good book contains more wealth than a good bank." Reading a book puts one in touch with an author the reader may never have a chance to meet in person, either because of distance or time. And reading is one of the best, most time-tested avenues to leadership experience. If other people's experience is the best teacher, books are the best transmitter of that experience.

Sometimes when we tout the benefits of reading, people assume we mean reading for entertainment. "Oh good!" they say. "I already read several novels a month." Certainly there is an entertainment value to reading. But when we speak of reading good books, we are not referring to the latest dime-store thriller that keeps one turning pages or to the type of books that can be "read in one sitting." Our reading should not just be for enjoyment, but should foster growth in our minds and persons. Reading should lead to better thoughts, which in turn lead to better actions, which then lead to better habits, which then produce better results, which then produce a better future.

As perhaps only Mark Twain could say, "The man who does not read good books has no advantage over the man who can't read them."

"Not all readers are _____, but all leaders must be
_____."

"The man who does not _____ _____
_____ has no advantage over the man who can't
_____ _____."

Why is reading important to growing your leadership influence?

_____

_____

_____

Does it matter *what* you are reading? Why?

_____

_____

_____

I will read _____ books this year.
          (number)

Possible titles:

_____

_____

_____

I will read _____ books this month.
          (number)

Possible titles:

_____

_____

_____

Leaders Learn from Audio Recordings

It is almost a universal rule that ambitious people are busy. The type of people who would invest the time to read a workbook on leadership certainly fit that description. So what is one of the most effective methods of learning on a continual basis in the midst of such a busy life? The answer is audio recordings.

In nearly every field of endeavor, audio recordings are available in various mediums or formats. They are convenient sources of learning and inspiration because they can be played almost anywhere a leader goes. Audio recordings also have the added benefit of teaching through what the listener hears. This involves a different set of brain functions than does reading. Some people learn more by what they see, while others learn more from what they hear. A steady diet of book reading and listening to audio recordings blends these two learning methods and maximizes the leader's education.

Leaders should search to find audio recordings produced by top performers in their field. By this method, leaders can take advantage of the principle of learning from the experience of others and actually learn from many mentors at once.

Great leaders know that "listening time" is not for entertainment, but for education. And true leaders take every advantage they can, accomplishing more than one thing at a time. There is a tremendous economy of time to be gained when listening to an audio recording while driving a car, taking a shower, or performing mindless chores. Leaders understand the power of passive education through listening and the advantages to be gained by multitasking as a way to optimize their educational opportunities.

Why is listening to audio recordings important to growing your leadership influence?

_____

_____

_____

Circle each activity you currently do during which it could be possible to listen to an audio recording.

Commuting for work   Getting ready in the morning
Transporting kids   Completing daily chores around the house
Traveling   Relaxing at home
Working   Fixing things around the house
Taking a lunch break   Getting ready for bed

I will listen to _____ recordings this year.
         (number)

I will listen to _____ recordings per month.
         (number)

I will listen to _____ recordings per week.
         (number)

I will listen to _____ recordings per day.
         (number)

Possible titles:

_____

_____

_____

Leaders Learn from Videos

Videos in large part combine the benefits of reading and listening to audio recordings, in that they provide something for both the visual and the auditory learner. Videos can also be an extremely clear form of communication where graphs, charts, photographs, and other forms of visuals are beneficial. Famous sales trainer and author Zig Ziglar said that over two-thirds of communication is "non-verbal." Videos help the learner capture the visual components of communication along with the audio ones, thereby enhancing comprehension.

Leaders pursue every avenue of learning available to them in their quest for increased leadership effectiveness, and that often includes a steady intake of instructional and informational videos.

Why is learning from videos important to growing your leadership influence?

_____

_____

_____

I will learn from _____ videos this year.
                    (number)

I will learn from _____ videos per month.
                    (number)

I will learn from _____ videos per week.
                    (number)

Possible titles:

_____

_____

_____

Leaders Learn from Association with Other Successful Leaders

"Birds of a feather flock together," goes the old saying. "Tell me who you hang around, and I'll tell you all about you," says another. "We are a product of the books we read, the things we listen to, and the people we associate with," says yet another. These sayings all ring with the same truth: that we become a lot like the people with whom we choose to associate. For this reason, leaders must seek out and associate with other leaders.

This can and should be done interpersonally, as well as through seminars and symposiums in the areas of leadership and in the leader's specific field. There is something magical about gathering with other like-minded leaders who are in pursuit of common goals. Attending seminars and conferences reinforces the leader's convictions and beliefs in his endeavor and builds relationships with other leaders that can last a lifetime and be mutually beneficial.

Robert Kiyosaki said, "Your income will be the average of the five people you hang around the most." But the most poignant story about the power of association comes from Mark Victor Hansen, co-author of the wildly popular *Chicken Soup for the Soul* book series. Earlier in his career, he had the opportunity to meet with success coach and author Tony Robbins. Robbins inquired as to the income level of the people Hansen associated with on a regular basis to discuss careers and share ideas. Hansen replied that the range was $5 million to $6 million per year. Robbins replied that everyone in his own group of affiliation earned around $100 million per year, and that explained their obvious difference in incomes!

While most of us don't start out having access to the fabulously successful, we can make every effort to read great books and attend conferences and seminars featuring those who have succeeded in our chosen field. It only makes sense that by associating with success, we will begin to understand the thinking behind that success more clearly.

Why is learning from association with other successful leaders important to growing your leadership influence?

_____

_____

_____

In the past, how have you selected your associations?

_____

_____

_____

What are the common characteristics found in the people with whom you surround yourself?

_____

_____

_____

Do the people you've chosen to spend time with enhance your life or make it more difficult?

_____

_____

_____

Evaluate your associations. List the names of your current inner circle. What qualities and skills do they bring to the table? In which areas are they better equipped than you? How do their abilities complement and complete your abilities? How do they support you emotionally? How do they move you closer to your goals for the team?

_____

_____

_____

Are some of your associations currently hindering your progress? What can you do to minimize or remove their influence?

_____

_____

_____

If they're doing more harm than good, how must you change your associations?

_____

_____

_____

I will attend _____ seminars/conferences this year.
          (number)

I will attend _____ seminars/conferences per month.
          (number)

The next seminar/conference I will attend is

_____.
          (date and location)

Do you already have access to an ongoing, credible educational program that provides leadership and personal-development books, recordings, videos, seminars, and conferences?

Leaders Learn from Coaches and Mentors

We have already discussed the many reasons why seeking counsel is critical in the growth and development of a leader. Credible coaches and mentors have what can be called "fruit on the tree," meaning that they have accomplished significantly in the areas in which a leader operates, or they have proven themselves adept at developing those in the leader's field. Andy Stanley writes in *The Next Generation Leader*, "You will never maximize your potential in any area without coaching. It is impossible. You may be good. You may even be better than everyone else. But without outside input, you will never be as good as you can be. We all do better when someone else is watching and evaluating."

There is a fine line of difference between the terms *coach* and *mentor* as we will be using them in this workbook. A coach is someone who encourages, guides, and develops the performance of another. A mentor is someone who helps mold and develop the very makeup and character of another. Leaders should seek and find credible coaches and mentors and utilize them on a regular basis as the cornerstone of their learning process.

A coach is someone who encourages, guides, and develops the _____ of another.

A mentor is someone who helps mold and develop the very _____ and _____ of another.

168 | HOW A LEADER GROWS IN INFLUENCE

What are some examples of what a coach might do with you compared to what a mentor would do?

_____

_____

_____

Do you currently have a coach or coaches in your life? If so, who? If not, list some possibilities.

_____

_____

_____

Do you currently have a mentor or mentors in your life? If so, who? If not, list some possibilities.

_____

_____

_____

Leaders Learn from Action

The methods of learning we've been discussing could be classified as theoretical in nature, but theory carries the learning process only so far. An old proverb says, "Do not let all your learning lead to knowledge; let it lead to action." Theory is not an education in itself; it is the warm-up for actual experience.

An apprentice once asked his master how he obtained such great wisdom.

"Wisdom comes from good judgment," answered the master.

"But how does one obtain good judgment?" asked the apprentice.

"By experiencing enough bad judgment," answered the master.

Theory actively *applied to experience* is a leader's best schoolmaster.

"Do not let all your learning lead to _____; let it lead to _____."

Theory actively applied to experience is a leader's best _____.

Leaders Learn by Controlling the Flow

Education does not merely consider what should be included but also focuses on what should be left out. This is called "controlling the flow." A leader closely controls the quality of what is allowed into his brain. On a daily basis there is an inundation of information and viewpoints, opinions, commentary, gossip, slander, libel, misinformation, propaganda, and just plain "junk food for the brain." It becomes necessary to filter out as much of what is not fruitful for growth as possible. This may involve the breaking of some bad habits, which could include too much television, news, newspapers, and talk radio. This is necessary for many reasons.

The Bible says, "Whatever is true, whatever is honorable, whatever is right, whatever is pure, whatever is lovely, whatever is of good repute, if there is any excellence and if anything worthy of praise, dwell on these things" (Philippians 4:8, NASB). Controlling the Flow is controlling the thoughts on which your mind dwells.

A leader closely controls the _____ of what is allowed into his _____.

Controlling the _____ is controlling the thoughts on which your mind dwells.

Summary

Leaders do not graduate from Level 1 and move up the Levels of Influence unless they have mastered the fundamentals of learning. Learning must become a consistent way of life if a leader is to survive. It is at this First Level of Influence that a leader develops and continues to develop the skills that will carry him or her throughout the challenges ahead. Through the learning process, the leader's competency should become obvious to all. It is when this begins happening that the leader advances to the Second Level of Influence.

CHAPTER 7

The Second Level of Influence: Performing

When your work speaks for itself, don't interrupt.

—HENRY J. KAISER

The second of the Five Levels of Influence is to become a Performer. If a leader never progressed beyond Level 1, she would not really accomplish much. That is because, more than any other level, the First Level is largely preparatory

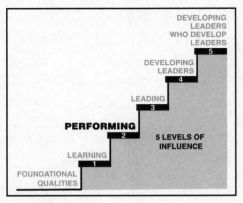

for the levels to come. It is at the Second Level where accomplishment begins. In this chapter, the terms *Level 2 Leader* and *Performance* will be used interchangeably.

At the Second Level of Influence, the child soccer player from the last chapter is now focusing on fundamental performance. She is continuing to learn, of course, but her top priority is scoring goals, blocking shots, and becoming a key player on her team.

Presuppositions or the "Art" of Performing

Becoming a Performer requires a certain mind-set. It starts with the correct presuppositions or mentalities. Proper thinking is the foundation of proper actions, and proper actions are what give birth to performance.

What does becoming a Performer require? _____ _____ _____ - _____

Performers Understand That Results Come through Personal Effort

At the Second Level of Influence, the leader's accomplishments are mostly her own. Her influence extends only as far as her own ability to perform, and no further. But the Second Level is critical and can have significant impact, as we will see. It is also a prerequisite to any Levels of Leadership that follow.

At the Second Level of Influence, the leader's _____ are mostly her own.

Performers Understand That Champions Don't Start Out That Way

For those new to the topic of success or leadership, it seems common to assume that champions have always been successful. Nothing could be a bigger myth. Champions become that way only through the commitment that follows a decision to be great. That commitment then gets applied to learning, growing, changing, performing, adjusting, and improving. Apply this formula, over time, with enthusiasm, and *that's* where champions originate. They do not start out that way.

Over and over again in the stories of achievers, we see that champions don't start out that way. As Monty Hall said, "Actually, I'm an overnight success. But it took twenty years!"

Champions become that way only through the _____ that follows a decision to be great.

Do you know any successful people that didn't start out that way? If so, explain.

_____

_____

_____

Performers Know There Will Be Many Opportunities to Feel Second Best

Sometimes people struggle to become Performers and find themselves smack up against a poor self-image. Additionally, there seems to be no shortage of situations that expose us to these feelings of inadequacy. We all have them. But Performers know they must succeed despite these feelings, not in the absence of them. It is a decision. To reach our potential, growth isn't optional. It is required. Performers take their feelings of inadequacy and turn them around, preferring to see them as measurements of their full potential.

To reach our potential, _____ isn't optional.

With what you have learned so far in this workbook, what are some ideas you can use to turn around feelings of inadequacy you may have?

_____

_____

_____

Performers Understand That Nothing Worthwhile Comes Easy

Success exacts a price, but it also delivers a prize. There will always be an exchange of effort for reward. Performers know that nothing good comes easily. Nor do they expect things to happen overnight. They know that success is always located on the other side of inconvenience.

Effort fully releases its reward only after a person refuses to quit. Persistence is the key. Robert Strauss said of success, "It's a little like wrestling a gorilla. You don't quit when you're tired—you quit when the gorilla is tired."

Success exacts a _____, but it also delivers a _____.

Success is always located on the other side of _____.

Effort fully releases its reward only after a person _____ _____ _____.

If you won at something with little to no effort, would it really feel like a success?

_____

Why do many lottery winners lose their winnings within a few years and end up further behind financially than before they bought the ticket?

_____

_____

_____

Performers Don't Expect Fair Treatment
Circle True or False.

True/False   Life is, and will always be, "not fair."

Watch any group of children playing, and it will be only a matter of time before one of them yells, "That's not fair." Even at a young age, we seem to have a sense of fair play, a sense of justice. Performers know that in life, there will be no shortage of situations that are "not fair." There will be no shortage of people who do us wrong, who cheat, lie, and steal, and who are just plain hurtful to others. Performers take this into account and strive for excellence anyway, focusing upon only what they can control.

On the wall of Mother Teresa's children's home in Calcutta was found the following inscription:

ANYWAY

People are unreasonable, illogical and self-centered.
LOVE THEM ANYWAY.
If you do good, people will accuse you of selfishness.
DO GOOD ANYWAY.
If you are successful, you will win false friends and true enemies.
SUCCEED ANYWAY.

The good you do will be forgotten tomorrow.
DO GOOD ANYWAY.
Honesty and frankness will make you vulnerable.
BE HONEST AND FRANK ANYWAY.
What you spend years building may be destroyed overnight.
BUILD ANYWAY.
People really need help but may attack you if you help them.
HELP PEOPLE ANYWAY.
Give the world the best you have, and you'll get kicked in the teeth.
GIVE THE WORLD THE BEST YOU'VE GOT ANYWAY.

Life is not fair, and sooner or later, that is true for everyone. Performers know this and win anyway.

Performers know that in life, there will be _____ _____ of situations that are "_____ _____."

Give the world the best you've got _____.

With the understanding that life is not fair, what can leaders do to still put the "odds" in their favor to win anyway?

_____

_____

_____

Performers Know There Will Always Be Critics

On the journey to success, the loudest sound a Performer may hear is the cries of critics. Critics are numerous and constant. They pop out of the woodwork anytime somebody tries to do anything worthwhile. Performers know this and learn to ignore their critics while remaining true to their vision and purpose. Learning to become a Performer must involve the growing of thick skin. As it has been said, the surest way to failure is to try to please everyone.

Learning to become a Performer must involve the growing of

_____ _____.

Why is it important to know there will always be critics and how to handle them?

_____

_____

_____

Performers Know There Will Always Be Strong Adversaries

Performers must develop the maturity to realize that there will always be a rival in opposition to their achievements. This rival may appear in the form of healthy competition for a certain position or achievement, or it may be someone committed to opposing your success and working to ensure your failure. As an Olympic athlete once said, "The competition is only there to keep me honest, ensuring that I extract the optimum performance from myself."

Performers must develop the _____ to realize that there will always be a _____ in opposition to their achievements.

How can competition or strong adversaries be a benefit to a Performer?

_____

_____

_____

Performers Understand That Breaks Will Come to Those Who Prepare

Success comes when opportunity and preparedness meet. It's what a person does when there are no outward results that determines the height of his or her greatness later. A Performer learns to prepare when there is no applause or positive feedback, relying on that day when the opportunity will come to make all the hard work pay off. Coach John Wooden said, "You must ... realize that [your] goal will be simply a by-product of all the hard work and good thinking you do along the way—your preparation. The preparation is where success is truly found."

The mark of a true Performer is perhaps best summarized by the lyrics in an old rock song: "When my ship rolls in, I'll be ready."

Success comes when _____ and _____ meet.

Performers Know That Attitude Conquers Circumstances

Attitude is paramount to understanding the performance of a leader. Zig Ziglar tells us, "Your attitude, not your aptitude, will determine your altitude." A leader's attitude is critical to his success. One of the keys to having and maintaining a positive attitude is to focus only on what you can control. As the saying goes, "There is no bad weather, just bad clothing!"

"Your _____, not your aptitude, will determine your _____."

"There is no bad weather, just bad _____!"

Do you think you can still be a successful leader with a bad attitude? Why?

_____

_____

_____

Most people who lose their jobs get fired due to their attitude. What is your reaction to this?

_____

_____

_____

Performers Understand That Desire Trumps Talent

Each individual comes into the world with a unique set of circumstances. Family lives, education, relationships, and physical characteristics are all different. Talent levels and opportunities vary. People are not the same in all things, but results can be equalized with effort. A person can't change his native abilities, but he can certainly control how he uses what he has.

People are not the same in all things, but results can be equalized with _____.

Performers Can Never Be Satisfied

As mentioned before, the very support structure of leadership is hunger: a strong productive desire to affect the status quo in a positive way. Ambition dies when satisfaction becomes too pervasive. As leaders perform and begin bringing their vision to reality, there will always be the temptation to become complacent or lazy, to give in to the satisfaction of a job well done. Performers are on guard against this and strive to maintain their hunger and grow their vision even bigger.

The very support structure of leadership is hunger: a strong productive _____ to affect the status quo in a _____ way.

Ambition dies when _____ becomes too pervasive.

Why is it important for leaders to never become satisfied?

_____

_____

_____

Performers Know There Is Power in Belief

In the book *What to Say When You Talk to Your Self*, author Shad Helmstetter tells us, "The brain simply believes what you tell it most. Whatever thoughts you have programmed into yourself, or have allowed others to program into you, are affecting, directing, or controlling everything about you." There seems to be a natural tendency for much of this "programming" to be negative in nature. Helmstetter continues: "If we grew up in fairly average, reasonably positive homes, we were told 'No!' or what we could not do, more than 148,000 times! As much as seventy-five percent or more of everything that is recorded and stored in our subconscious minds is counterproductive and works against us—in short, we are programmed *not* to succeed!" Perhaps this is why so many people never develop as leaders and find success elusive. What we believe will happen and what actually does happen are largely one and the same. There is a self-fulfilling quality to both worry and optimism. Winners choose the power of belief in a positive outcome. David Schwartz says, "Believe, really believe you can succeed, and you will."

There is power in belief. Beliefs control realities. Belief compels leaders to reach for what may seem unattainable to others. It allows people to push beyond the seemingly impossible. It pulls people through when all the evidence would suggest they should quit. Performers learn to foster a strong set of beliefs that enable them to do what they do. Good things normally occur to those who believe that they will!

The brain simply _____ what you tell it most.

What we _____ will happen and what actually does _____ are largely one and the same.

"Believe, really _____ you can _____, and you will!"

Why is there so much power in belief?

_____

_____

_____

What can keep people from harnessing the power of belief?

_____

_____

_____

What can you do to increase your belief at times when it may be hard?

_____

_____

_____

Actions or the "Science" of Performing

After achieving a firm understanding of the presuppositions grow-ing leaders must comprehend to become Performers, it is appro-priate to delve into the *actions* of performing, or the "science" side of what becoming a Performer is all about.

Performers Work as Part of an Overall Team

Leaders at Level 2 must recognize that they will accomplish more by being part of an overall team than they ever could on their own. Ray Kroc, founder of McDonald's Corporation, said, "None of us is as important as all of us." And then there is the famous acronym: TEAM, Together Everyone Achieves More.

"None of us is as important as _____ _____ _____."

Have you experienced the power of working as a team? If so, how did it affect your results?

_____

_____

Performers Edify the Organization's Leadership

Along with realizing their role in the larger team structure, leaders becoming Performers should edify the leadership of the organiza-tion. What does it mean to edify? In this usage, it means to "lift others up" through words and respect. This doesn't mean some strange sort of worship or idolatry. Edification of the leaders in authority above him is simply how a Performer amplifies his work and strengthens the bonds of the overall team. It is also how he shows respect. Edification can be done by praising with words, showing respect through actions, and taking care to advertise the accomplishments of the leadership. This is important because it sets the stage for how the developing leader will be treated by his followers as he ascends the Levels of Influence on his own journey. If a developing leader consistently seeks the good in the organization's leadership and amplifies that message, it will come back to him in droves.

Edify means to "lift others up" through _____ and _____.

Why is it important for Performers to edify the leadership in their organization?

_____

_____

_____

How do you feel when someone advertises your accomplishments in front of others?

_____

_____

_____

If you see your mentor or someone you respect advertise the accomplishments of somebody, does your view of that somebody change? Explain.

_____

_____

_____

Performers Promote the Training System and Learning Environment

Leaders at the Performer Level must also embrace the training system and learning environment of their organization. This means not only taking full advantage of it for themselves, but also becoming promoters of it to others in the organization. In this way, a Performer *amplifies* his energy throughout the organization and empowers others to learn and grow also. Promoting means helping others understand the benefits of something. There is a proper way to do this, and it involves three steps:

1. Announce
2. Explain
3. Promote

When promoting a facet of the training system, leaders should first announce it clearly. Announcements simply include all the facts about something, such as the what, when, and where. Next, leaders should explain the event or training aid in enough detail to communicate any background information that will help the listener understand exactly what is being promoted. Finally, leaders should promote by highlighting the relevance of the item for the listener. Remember, the number one thing most people care about when hearing about something new is: What's in it for me? This is where it is helpful if leaders have taken the time to get to know the people around them, as covered previously. In such cases, leaders can promote specifically to the needs and abilities of the listener, thereby ensuring the relevance of the message.

A key to promotion is the concept of "uniqueness." When promoting any facet of the organization, the leader must first ask: What is unique about this? Perhaps it is the first time such an event has been held, or perhaps it is the last. Maybe it is a brand-new training technique but has already received wonderful results. Whatever the case, leaders look for uniqueness before they begin to promote. This adds value to the promotion and increases relevance to the listener.

The three steps of promotion are: 1. _____
2. _____ 3. _____.

The number one thing most people care about when hearing about something new is: _____ in it _____ _____?

What would the positive results be if the leader was able to promote the training system and learning environment well?

_____

_____

_____

Performers Follow the Proven Methods

There are certain techniques and strategies for every organization and endeavor that have been proven, over time, to work. There is a time and a place for innovation and even radical change, but it is not at this level. If a leader has not proven mastery of the basic strategies and patterns, he has no ground to stand on when attempting to initiate change.

Remember, leadership is influence. If a leader has no record of performance, that leader will have no influence. The quickest, most assured way of gaining that track record of performance is to absolutely master the patterns of success already established in an organization.

If a leader has no record of _____, that leader will have no _____.

Why is it important for a leader to master the proven methods before trying to innovate?

_____

_____

_____

Performers Build on Their Basic Strengths

If people are not created equal in all things, then it only follows that people are unequal in different things. This means that some are better in some areas than others. Performers learn to use their strengths to gain success while working in the background to minimize the shortcomings of their weaknesses. Nobody is good at everything, but everyone is good at *something*. Success comes from identifying what your *strengths* are and building on them.

Nobody is good at _____, but everyone is good at _____.

What are you currently good at? What are some of your strengths?

_____

_____

_____

Performers Initiate Activity

Leaders absolutely must be self-starters. That is why we spent so much time covering the various types of motivation earlier in this workbook. Leaders must know what makes them tick, and they must wind the mechanisms of that clock on a regular basis. Often, growing leaders ask their mentors if they will do one thing or another to help them stay motivated; a wise mentor will answer that although he may be willing, he knows he would fail miserably. There is no source of external circumstances that can be relied upon to provide consistent motivation to a Performer. It is an internal job. Leaders must embrace this truth and strive daily to motivate themselves to take initiative, be self-starting, and perform.

Leaders absolutely must be _____ -_____.

Motivation is an _____ job.

Performers Push to Grow and Improve

No one has ever accomplished great things by babying himself. Along with taking personal initiative, leaders must learn to push themselves beyond the borders of their comfort zone. What is a comfort zone? It is the fictitious area of activity in which a person feels comfortable. It is fictitious because the concept of familiarity is actually being confused with "comfort." A more accurate term would be the *familiar* zone. How many leaders are really *comfortable* in their normal activities? We have already established that would-be leaders start with a discontent with the status quo. The terms *comfort* and *leadership* are at war with one another, so for a leader, there can't actually be a comfort zone.

This idea of a familiar zone is real. The challenge becomes stepping beyond the familiar or easy. That is the very task of a leader: to take people where, many times, even the leader has never been. To do this, leaders must embrace the idea of being uncomfortable and in unfamiliar territory on a regular basis. When leaders stop getting outside of their familiar zone, they cease to be leaders.

It is okay and even necessary for a leader to push himself. The rewards for achievement hide themselves beyond the borders of the familiar zone, awaiting those with the guts and the discipline to push hard, experience personal growth, improve, act with courage, and go places not gone before to claim those rewards as their prize.

No one has ever accomplished great things by _____ himself.

A more accurate term for comfort zone would be the _____ zone.

What are some things you can do to get outside of your familiar zone today? This week? This month? This year?

_____

_____

_____

Performers Become Relatable

Here we see again the importance of the people skills the leader learned in Level 1: In order to maximize his influence, a leader must be relatable. This means being likable, being sincere, and dealing with people in a "low friction" way. People who leave a trail of broken relationships and hurt feelings or who lash out at others or act bossy rarely have any real influence with people. Leaders must take an active interest in others by inquiring, listening, smiling, and caring. These qualities make the leader relatable to others and build trust—and trust is the foundation of relationships. Only with these bonds can leaders wield any influence in the lives of others.

Why is getting along with others especially important for leaders?

_____

_____

_____

Performers Become Believable and Demonstrate Conviction

Leaders gain credibility with their organizations by fostering trust and demonstrating a history of performance. But they also do it through their conviction. In many cases, the leader's vision will be larger and farther reaching than that held by most of the organization. For this reason, it may be difficult for followers to believe in the vision of the leader; it is beyond their grasp. It is not important that people believe in the vision, but they must believe the leader believes in it! Followers can run on the leader's conviction until they gain their own. Leaders must demonstrate conviction with both words and actions.

Why must the followers buy in to the leader before they buy in to the vision?

_____

_____

_____

Performers Maintain a Positive Attitude

The mark of a great Performer is a positive attitude. Mature leaders understand that it is not what happens to them but how they respond that counts. Stephen Covey, author of *The Seven Habits of Highly Effective People*, explains that between stimulus and response we have a choice of how we are going to react. We are response-able, i.e., responsible. That is where good attitudes come from: knowing we have a choice in the matter and making the mature choice to maintain a cheery outlook no matter what happens.

One reason attitude is so important is because it is contagious. Have you ever known someone who has a sour disposition to walk into a room and bring everybody down? They are called "sunshine people"—the room brightens when they leave! Or, conversely, have you ever noticed how contagious a smile can be? We all know people who smile readily and just always seem to be cheery. Whether uplifting or discouraging, attitudes are contagious—and a positive attitude is much more productive than a negative one.

Another reason attitudes of leaders are so important is because they are of a self-fulfilling nature. There is a gravestone in England that reads, "SEE, I TOLD YOU I WAS SICK." Attitudes are like that. They tend to produce what we command of them. We don't get what we want, and we don't get what we deserve, but we usually get what we expect. Attitude plays a big part in determining what we expect to happen.

People with positive attitudes just simply seem to outperform people with poor attitudes. For no other reason than pragmatism, leaders should work to keep their attitudes high because sooner or later, the man who wins is the man who thinks he can.

The mark of a great Performer is a _____ _____.

Mature leaders understand that it is not what happens to them, but how they _____ that counts.

People with _____ attitudes just simply seem to outperform people with _____ attitudes.

How often do you let your emotions and attitude get the best of you? Which emotions (examples: anger, sadness, pride) are the most difficult for you to handle appropriately?

_____

_____

_____

List some specific ways you can begin to limit the ways these emotions limit you.

_____

_____

_____

Do you tend to see situations through positive or negative eyes?

_____

_____

_____

How can altering your perspective change how you handle situations?

_____

_____

_____

Do any of your past experiences continue to haunt you with bitterness or anger? If so, what can you do to let go of that negative attitude and move forward?

_____

_____

_____

Do any of your followers have negative attitudes? Can any aspect of that be traced back to your attitude?

_____

_____

_____

192 | HOW A LEADER GROWS IN INFLUENCE

What resources will you read or listen to in order to help your attitude?

_____

_____

_____

Performers Give Their Best in Every Situation

It is a natural tendency to blame performance in life on circumstances. "I had a bad childhood," says one. "I've been discriminated against," says another. "I wasn't given the talents those others have." These excuses are all too common. Performers know that it is not what happens but how they respond that leads to greatness. It doesn't matter where you start; it matters how you finish. Talent and wealth and connections and luck can certainly give a person a head start, but almost always, the victory goes to the most determined and committed. President Calvin Coolidge said it best:

> Press on.
> Nothing in the world can take the place of persistence.
> Talent will not.
> Nothing is more common than unsuccessful men with talent.
> Genius will not.
> Unrewarded genius is almost a proverb.
> Education alone will not.
> The world is full of educated derelicts.
> Persistence and determination alone are omnipotent.

It is a natural tendency to _____ performance in life on circumstances.

Performers know that it is not what _____ but how they _____ that leads to greatness.

It doesn't matter where you _____; it matters how you _____.

"Persistence and determination alone are _____."

Performers Focus on Priorities

As detailed in the Cycle of Achievement, productivity comes from focus. Performers often accomplish so much because they bring all their energies to bear upon a single point of interest.

Lou Holtz represents this principle with the acronym WIN, which stands for "What's Important Now?" Performers must keep that question in mind so they can focus their energies on the one most important thing at a given moment. Most people try to do too much with too little focus and end up accomplishing next to nothing. Performers focus on priorities and concentrate their energies on the best things to do, leaving the good things for another time.

WIN = What's Important _____?

Performers Get Results (Execute)

All of these attributes of leaders in the performance stage are important, but everything eventually comes down to results. Leaders must be effective. As our friend Larry VanBuskirk says, "It can't be a try." Or as the character Yoda from the *Star Wars* movies said, "There is no try, only do."

You can always tell the real leaders because their teams consistently turn in superior performances. Leaders must avoid the pitfalls of appearing busy but having little to show for it, hoping somehow to act and look the part but never quite delivering the goods.

Author James A. Autry said the key comment is, "I see you've been busy. Now tell me what you've accomplished." This is especially important at this stage in the Levels of Influence. If a leader does not learn to accomplish goals at this level, there will be no advancement to the next and no increase in influence.

Leaders must be _____.

Why is getting results a major part of leadership—especially at the Second Level of Influence?

_____

_____

_____

How can someone be really busy yet never accomplish much?

_____

_____

_____

In your home life or work, what are the top two things you need to accomplish today? This week? This month?

_____

_____

_____

Performers Ignore Their Press Clippings

A close cousin to complacency is arrogance. As leaders perform and success follows, there will be recognition and rewards. It is important not to get too puffed up with one's success or "read the press clippings." Performers know they are no better than any-body else, and they guard against the pitfalls of ego and arrogance. This is most easily done by remembering that the opportunities and abilities to perform in one's field are gifts from God. Such an outlook not only prevents arrogance but also fosters a spirit of gratefulness.

It is important not to get too _____ up with one's success or "read the _____ _____."

What can happen if a leader becomes arrogant about his or her abilities and results?

_____

_____

_____

What are some ways to stay humble and not fall into this trap?

_____

_____

_____

Summary

Would-be leaders making their way up the Five Levels of Influence and becoming Performers (Level 2 Leaders) will embody each of the steps in this chapter while continuing to follow the principles of learning we outlined in Level 1.

Becoming a Performer is a prerequisite to becoming a leader. *Again, becoming a Performer* must *happen before one can become a real leader.* It is performance that gives the budding leader credibility and influence and the ability to actually begin the calling of a leader—which is, of course, leading! Many, many would-be leaders miss this crucial step of becoming a Performer themselves. They assume that if they are given a position or act with authority, people will follow them. What they fail to realize is that they are then managing, not leading. There is a world of difference between the two. Only when one becomes an obvious Performer do others give one permission to truly *Lead*. Then it's time for Level 3.

CHAPTER 8

The Third Level of Influence: Leading

Being a general calls for talents different than those of a soldier.
—Titus Livy

So far, we have discussed ways a leader grows personally; now, it is time to deal specifically with the budding leader's ability to increase in influence through the leadership of other people. The leader thus far has made

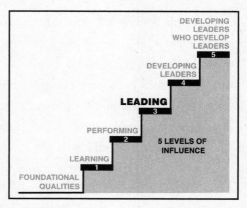

Learning a habit, has gained valuable experience becoming a high Performer, and is now ready to take responsibility for the Leadership of others. At this level, the group grows when and because the Leader is present. When capitalized, the term "Leader" will refer to a Level 3 Leader.

The soccer player from the previous two chapters is now becoming an on-field Leader of the other players. She is named team captain and, while playing the game herself, also organizes set pieces and directs activities.

Presuppositions or the "Art" of Leading

Just as with the previous step of becoming a Performer, becoming a Leader requires a certain mind-set. This is because Leadership itself is a perspective; it is the lens through which a person views the world. Leaders learn to see things a certain way, from a certain vantage point, so they can take responsibility for achievement through the efforts of a unified group of people.

Leadership itself is a _____; it is the _____ through which a person views the world.

Leaders Understand That Results Come through Team Effort

Leadership is how a Performer extends his or her ability through the efforts of others, to the betterment of everyone involved. In every situation, the Leader thinks in terms of "team" efforts and what resources he or she can pull together to get the job done. At Level 3, the working concept is no longer what the individual can do, but rather what a *team* of individuals can do.

This concept could be called "leverage." To explore this further, let's return to the equation we used in an earlier chapter:

$$Work = Force \times Distance$$

Or, as we modified it:

$$Influence = Effort \times Scope$$

The equation reveals that, assuming leaders have maximized their Effort, the only remaining way to increase Influence is through increasing Scope. There is a mechanical advantage gained by a leader orchestrating the efforts of a group of people to accomplish some larger task. When this is done properly, leaders amplify the power of individuals beyond the sum of the parts. As the saying goes, individuals can flourish but teams explode.

Consider again Bill Gates, billionaire founder of Microsoft Corporation and one of the world's richest individuals. How did Bill Gates's ideas for software for computers explode into such a large industry and an enormous fortune? There are many answers to this, of course, but one that can describe it as well as any is the concept of leverage.

Software is nothing more than a computer program. The cost of the actual product transferred to the customer is very little. In the case of an optical disc, it may be only a few dollars; in the case of an Internet download, radically less. The program was constructed one time and then copied millions of times. A term that describes this multiplication of results is *duplication*. That largely explains the enormous multiplier on Microsoft's income stream. Build a program once, duplicate it cheaply, and sell it millions of times. This is well beyond what Gates and his employees could do individually. For such enormous impact, they have to use the power of leverage.

Leadership works the same way. Leadership amplifies the reach or scope of a Performer through the joint efforts of other people. Without leadership, a person is limited to his or her own personal performance. We might say that a Level 2 Leader deals in addition, while a Level 3 Leader gains the leverage of multiplication.

Individuals can flourish, but teams _____.

Without leadership, a person is limited to his or her own
_____ _____.

Why can a team achieve multiple times the results of several individuals?

_____

_____

_____

Think of another example where a team was able to accomplish much more than if they had tried to work separately as individuals.

_____

_____

_____

Leaders Understand That People Buy In to the Leader before Anything Else

A critical presupposition all leaders must realize is that followers buy in to the leader before anything else. The vision may be compelling, but is the leader worth following? Can the leader be trusted? Opportunities may be enormous, but does the leader know what he or she is doing? These are the qualifying questions followers ask subconsciously before giving permission to be led.

Leadership is not a position or title; it is a condition of permission given by followers once they buy in to the leader. Leadership influence, like trust, must be earned and earned continually.

Leadership is not a _____ or _____;
it is a condition of _____ given by followers once they buy in to the leader.

Do you agree that people buy in to the leader before anything else? Why?

_____

_____

_____

Whose vision have you bought in to? What is it about the leader that makes him or her worth following?

_____

_____

_____

When might a follower look for another leader?

_____

_____

_____

Why might you stay with a leader, even when the person's initial vision departs from what it was when you began following him or her?

_____

_____

_____

Have you ever tried to cast a vision and not had people buy in to it and follow? How might your leadership have affected the response you received? Explain.

_____

_____

_____

Up to now, did you approach leadership with the understanding that people must first buy in to you before they will buy in to your vision? Give an example of your previous leadership approach to casting a vision and rallying followers.

_____

_____

_____

Leaders Understand the Importance of Finding and Developing Good People

Since the whole concept of leadership is the leverage of accomplishment through the collective efforts of a group of people, it stands to reason that the quality of the output will be directly related to the quality of the people involved. As we said earlier, finding and developing the *right* people is critical to the success of an endeavor. This is why attracting, training, and retaining people of high caliber is always a major consideration for a leader.

Finding and equipping others will consume an enormous amount of a leader's time but, as we have seen through the discussion on leverage, it will be more than worth it. Level 3 Leaders are only as good as their people.

Finding and developing the _____ people is critical to the success of an endeavor.

Why is it important to find and develop good people?

_____

_____

_____

Leaders Understand That Dealing with Inadequate Resources Is Common

While it may be important to lead people of the highest quality possible, most Leaders will find themselves severely lacking in this area. One of the realities of leadership is that there are no perfect teams. No matter how much effort and focus a leader puts upon finding and training people, there will always be deficiencies, and many times, those deficiencies will be enormous. Additionally, there will often be a severe lack of other resources, too. The leader who waits for an abundance of resources before setting out to accomplish a task is no leader at all. Reality for a leader is almost always a situation of lack and want. True Leaders understand this and make do the best they can anyway. As the saying goes, "If you wait for all the lights to turn green before you set off on a cross-country trip, you'll never leave."

One of the realities of leadership is that there are no _____ teams.

Reality for a leader is almost always a situation of _____ and _____.

Should leaders wait to take action until they have the best resources in order? Why?

_____

_____

_____

Leaders Understand That Leadership Is the Limitation

Author Ken Blanchard wrote, "No organization will rise above the passion of the leader." Leaders cannot blame their people, their resources, or their circumstances. The effectiveness of the Leader is the limitation upon the organization.

Leadership is not something that can be faked, although people frequently attempt it. Perhaps an individual has a title or position, so he thinks that gives him influence over others. Maybe somebody has achieved things in the past and figures those accomplishments provide influence today. While both of these assumptions may be true to some extent, leadership is earned on a continual basis. Followers look around and know who the real Leaders are in any given situation. This is why it is so critical that a leader is both an ongoing Learner and Performer. Learning, growing, and achieving build up a balance in the "bank account of credibility" with followers. The more a leader leads and the better his or her leadership, the higher the caliber of the followers he or she attracts and the better they perform. The better they perform, the better results the organization achieves. Through this process, the leader develops his or her people to grow personally and increase their personal effectiveness.

"No organization will rise above the _____ of the leader."

The more a leader _____ and the better his or her _____, the higher the caliber of the followers he or she attracts and the better they _____.

Why is an organization limited by the abilities and actions of the leader?

_____

_____

_____

If an organization isn't growing or performing, whose fault is it?

_____

_____

_____

Leaders Understand the Impact of Their Actions on the Organization

Level 3 Leaders must be cognizant that their every action has a reaction. There are many connection points to the organization when a Leader is responsible for a group of people. Selfishness, pettiness, and similar malfunctions of a Leader will stop his or her progress cold. Everything a Leader does is amplified now because he does it with and through his people. The ability to think in terms of a bigger picture and live by priorities is critical. At this level, good judgment and a positive attitude pay big dividends.

Everything a Leader does is _____ now because he does it with and through his _____.

Leaders Understand That Leadership Is about Sacrifice

Leadership is not a bed of roses. It is not something to be sought after for the purpose of perks and privilege. Leadership is about service to others. Leadership is a responsibility that demands self-discipline and sacrifice. As a matter of fact, the higher a leader rises, the less tolerance there is for error. Followers are checking all the time to see if the leader is "walking the walk" or just "talking the talk." Failings that may have been ignored at lower levels become poison once someone starts to Lead. This is because everything a Leader does is amplified through his or her organization and because now, the Leader is not just dealing with his or her own life but also the lives of others. This is a great responsibility.

There are definitely perks and privileges that come with successful leadership, and they are enjoyable and flattering. But these rewards are not the purpose of leadership; they are merely the side benefits. A Level 3 Leader will sacrifice personal desires for the good of the vision and the team. As a Leader puts his or her self-interests aside, learns to serve others and work toward the vision, and sacrifices for a purpose and a cause greater than himself, the rewards go beyond mere perks and trappings of success. The most important rewards become the satisfaction of seeing other people's lives enriched and the vision accomplished. Such deep and truly meaningful rewards make all the sacrifice worth it.

Leadership is a _____ that demands self-discipline and _____.

A Level 3 Leader will sacrifice personal _____ for the good of the _____ and the team.

The most important _____ become the satisfaction of seeing other people's lives enriched and the _____ accomplished.

Why is sacrifice a large part of leadership?

_____

_____

_____

Why is leadership worth the price of self-discipline and sacrifice?

_____

_____

_____

Leaders Understand That a Leader's Job Is Never Done

Leadership is not a "nine-to-five" operation. It does not neatly pack itself into a schedule. Leadership requires constancy and diligence and continual pondering. At no point in the leadership journey does a leader have the luxury of sitting back and thinking "I've arrived" or "I've got it all under control." The moment that happens, and maybe even sooner, the leader will be run over by problems or competition or both. There will always be new challenges and competitors and obstacles and opportunities. Nothing stands still, and leadership greatness is certainly no exception.

Great Leaders learn to find a defeat in every victory and a victory in every defeat. What does this mean? First of all, no matter how well a leader and his or her organization perform, there is always room for improvement. This attitude keeps leaders sharp and away from the dangerous Ditch of Complacency. On the other hand, sometimes leaders suffer through defeat after defeat. During those times—and they are likely to come sooner or later—great leaders look for signs of good in an otherwise bleak landscape.

Nothing stands _____, and leadership greatness is certainly no _____.

Great Leaders learn to find a _____ in every victory and a _____ in every defeat.

What might happen if a leader decides to sit back and not continue to get better?

_____

_____

_____

Think of a recent "victory" you had. What are some areas where you could have done better?

_____

_____

_____

Think of a recent "defeat" you had. What are some positive points involved in this situation?

_____

_____

_____

Actions or the "Science" of Leading

With these presuppositions in mind, it is appropriate to explore what leaders actually do at this Third Level of Influence. That's what the "science" side of leadership is all about.

Leaders Model the Way

To harness the collective energies of a group of people effectively, one must first model the way. There is no shortcut here. Of all the action steps (or "science") of leadership that follow, none of them matter if the master copy is not worth duplicating. One question to ask yourself is this: Would I want an entire organization filled with people just like me? If the answer is yes, then you are setting a good example and modeling the way (or you are terribly self-deceived).

Currently, would you be excited or frustrated if you had an organization filled with people just like you?

_____

_____

_____

Leaders Compel Individuals to Perform

A major job of a Level 3 Leader is to inspire others to perform and achieve results. The things that get accomplished are the things that get rewarded. Outstanding performance must be recognized and rewarded, and this should be done publicly. This communicates a standard to the rest of the organization for which others can strive and motivates the star performers to reach even greater heights.

Outstanding performance must be _____ and _____, and this should be done _____.

In your organization, what are the top three things that people should be recognized and rewarded for doing?

_____

_____

_____

This week, catch three people in the act of doing something right and publicly recognize them.

Who were the three people?

1. _____
2. _____
3. _____

What did you observe each of them doing right?

1. _____

2. _____

3. _____

How did you recognize their performance?

1. _____

2. _____

3. _____

What was their reaction to the recognition?

1. _____

2. _____

3. _____

Leaders Coach Others

As we said before, leaders function as coaches. Coaching involves increasing the performance of one's individual team members and getting them to work together effectively.

Leaders at this Level of Influence are responsible and qualified to coach those at the previous two levels. This is one of the reasons it is so important for a leader to master each of the previous Levels of Influence. A leader doesn't really know how well he knows something until he tries to teach it.

Coaching involves _____ the _____ of individual team members and getting them to work _____ effectively.

Leaders Become Servants

Leaders must learn that to lead means to serve. Leadership is not about position or perks or status. It is not about power or wealth. It is about service to others expanded through the coordinated efforts of people. The single most effective way for a leader to get the most out of his organization is to serve its people.

A leader shows his love for his team and serves them in their efforts to perform. By serving others, a Level 3 Leader maximizes the performance of his or her team.

Leaders must learn that to lead means to _____.

Why is service to others so important to understand in leadership? Aren't leaders supposed to be the ones being served? Explain.

_____

_____

_____

Looking back, did the people who had the most positive influence in your life (leaders) also have a servant's heart? Explain.

_____

_____

_____

Leaders Operate as Field Commanders

At Level 3, Leaders exert influence through actually being there in person. They are in the fight with their troops, so to speak, and are on hand to observe and direct activities. They can see changes in conditions and orchestrate accordingly. Their presence is reassuring to their people, and inspiration and vision are given firsthand. It is also here that the leader realizes very quickly that the speed of the group is the speed of the leader. Since the Leader is up close and personal with his people, his performance has a big impact on the overall team's performance. Leadership by example is crucial at Level 3 and above. Personal charisma, people skills, relationships, and rapport make the Level 3 Leader especially effective.

When Leaders are with their followers in person, inspiration and
_____ can be given firsthand, and their presence is
_____ to their people.

Some see leadership as someone giving orders to an organization
from afar. Does this common perception correlate with true, effective leadership? Why?

_____

_____

_____

Leaders Orchestrate Activity

Orchestration involves seeing the things that need to be done and
coordinating people's efforts in that direction. Leaders must learn
to put the right people in the right places. Jim Collins, in his book
Good to Great, talks about first having the right people on the bus.
Then he stresses the importance of having the right people in the
right seats on that bus. Both are critical to a Leader's orchestration of his team and demonstrate once again the importance of a
Leader knowing his players. These players have strengths and abilities in certain areas that should be utilized accordingly. Individual
attention and knowledge multiplies a Level 3 Leader's effectiveness
with his or her team.

Leaders must learn to put the right _____ in the right
_____.

Should Leaders treat all their people the same? Why?

_____

_____

_____

Why is it important to not only have the right people but to have them in the right places?

_____

_____

_____

Leaders Measure Results

Level 3 is about team *results*, and Level 3 Leaders keep score. As with any sporting event, there is a scoreboard for an organization. (And if there isn't, there should be.) Leaders must learn to keep score so they can accurately measure the performance of their team and therefore glean concrete feedback on their own performance as a Leader. At Level 3, Leaders measure results, confront brutal reality, and take steps toward improvement. Anything less is negligence of duty.

Level 3 is about team _____, and Level 3 Leaders keep _____.

If you currently keep score of the results within your organization, what are the top three things you track?

1. _____
2. _____
3. _____

Why are these three things important to track?

_____

_____

_____

If you do not currently keep score of the results within your organization, what three things should you track from this point forward?

1. _____

2. _____

3. _____

Why are these three things important to track?

_____

_____

_____

Leaders Solve Problems

Being a problem solver requires courage. Leaders must face challenges head-on and without delay. Problems are much easier to kill when they are small.

Certain situations resemble forest fires and require the leader to throw water on them and douse the flames. Others appear as small embers of possibility and require the leader to pour on some gasoline and incite progress. Successful Third Level Leaders know what is needed and when. They become adept at solving problems and, eventually, even heading problems off at the pass and dousing them before they blossom into full-scale conflagrations.

Problems are much easier to kill when they are _____.

Can you think of an example of a problem that grew into a large flame because no one doused it with water when it was little? What happened?

_____

_____

_____

How should this problem have been dealt with earlier?

_____

_____

_____

Can you think of an example of a small ember of possibility that was doused with water when the gasoline of encouragement should have been poured on it instead? What was the result?

_____

_____

_____

Leaders Communicate

A leader must be a good communicator. The more aggressive the tasks of the team, the more the leader must communicate. When people are informed, they feel a sense of security and shared ownership in the objectives. When communication is poor, they feel distrust and a lack of closeness. Poor communication breeds friction and trouble. Proper Level 3 Leadership begins, continues, and ends with good communication.

The more aggressive the _____ of the team, the more the leader must _____.

Why is communication so important in leadership?

_____

_____

_____

What are some ways that can help the communication of a Leader?

_____

_____

_____

Summary

As a leader comes to understand the presuppositions (art) of Level 3 Leadership and habitually execute the actions (science) of Level 3, he or she will rise in influence. Such a Leader will be able to achieve tremendously more significant and sizable results than anything accomplished by performing personally, while enriching the lives of others in the process. However, at this Third Level of Influence the leverage involved only goes as far as the Leader's personal reach. That influence is a product of the Leader's presence on the scene. But the principles of leadership embodied on the Third Level are amplified in Level 4 as the Leader learns to have influence not just through a band of *followers*, but through the development and effectiveness of *other Leaders*.

CHAPTER 9

The Fourth Level of Influence:
Developing Leaders

A leader is best when people barely know he exists. Not so good when people obey and acclaim him. Worse when they despise him. But of a good leader who talks little when his work is done, his aim fulfilled, they will say, "We did it ourselves."

—LAO-TZU (604-531 B.C.)

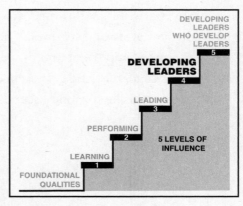

The fourth of the Five Levels of Influence is Developing Leaders. This level deals with the leader's ability to increase his influence through the development of other leaders. The leader continues to Learn (Level 1), Perform (Level 2), and Lead (Level 3), but now develops others who can also thrive at each of those three levels.

At Level 4, the group grows because the leader has grown other Level 3 Leaders. A Level 4 Leader is basically in the business of replacing himself.

Continuing with the example of the soccer player in previous chapters, at Level 4, she has become head coach. Her influence does not stem from her position, though. Rather, it comes from her ability to develop other player-leaders (team captains, etc.) and assistant coaches. Her abilities are employed to develop others into leadership positions within the sport. These individuals seek her mentorship and guidance to aid them in growing their own abilities to lead.

A Level 4 Leader is basically in the business of _____ himself.

Presuppositions or the "Art" of Leadership Development

As with each of the previous Levels of Influence, there are some vital presuppositions at the step of Developing Other Leaders. Once the presuppositions are right in the mind of the leader, then the correct actions will follow.

There is also a subtle trend at work as we progress upward through the Levels of Influence. The higher a leader goes up the steps, the more important and numerous the *presuppositions*, while at the same time, the actual *actions* become smaller and fewer. Said another way, the higher one ascends the Levels, the more "art"

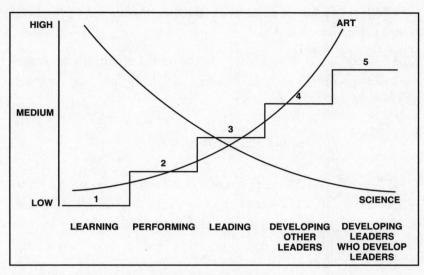

and less "science" is required. Who one *is* becomes much more important than what one *does*. Don't get us wrong, leaders will be busy and work hard at each of the Five Levels of Influence, but the emphasis of their efforts will change along with their growth in ability.

The higher one ascends the levels, the more "_____" and less "_____" is required.

As you ascend the Levels of Influence, why do you think it is more important who you are than what you do?

_____

_____

_____

Level 4 Leaders Know Results Will Come through the Efforts of Other Leaders

This Fourth Level is significant because it dramatically increases the leader's scope or range. Let's refer back to the physical equation once again:

$$Influence = Effort \times Scope$$

Where a Level 3 Leader benefited from the concepts of leverage in terms of *multiplication* (coordinating the efforts of a unified team of performers), the Level 4 Leader gains the advantages of *exponential* growth (developing other leaders who each deal in *multiplication*).

Level 4 Leaders Understand the Power of Duplication

Circle True or False.

True/False   If you want something done right, you have to do it yourself.

Whereas a Level 3 Leader must be present with his or her team in order to achieve success, Level 4 Leaders get results even when they are not around. This effectiveness obtained through the output of *other leaders* generates a result we call duplication. Duplication is the reason for the exponential growth discussed in the previous paragraph.

Level 4 Leaders confront challenges and opportunities by asking themselves questions such as: Whom have I developed who can handle this? Which of my leaders has a team capable of taking on this task? What have I done or what can I do to help this leader or that leader grow and improve?

Level 4 Leaders are able to align with other leaders in common purpose. Then they develop those leaders to be able to achieve team success even when the Level 4 Leader is not around. The result is productivity that compounds exponentially.

Level 4 Leaders get _____ even when they are not around.

How would you go about choosing someone to replace yourself?

_____

_____

_____

Level 4 Leaders Know That Leaders Have Strengths in Various Areas

Level 4 Leaders are not "turf protectors" or "glory hogs" who have to be the best at everything, get the glory for every accomplishment, and be in on every decision. Level 4 Leaders surround themselves with leaders who have strengths in various areas and, in many cases, strengths in areas where the Level 4 Leader is weak. In other words, Level 4 Leaders care more about the vision than their own personal glory. They know that they are not great at everything, so they bring along other leaders who are good in areas where they are not. And they also bring along leaders who are strong where they are strong and are not intimidated by them.

Level 4 Leaders care more about the _____ than their own personal glory.

Level 4 Leaders Know the Vision Must Be Big Enough for Many Leaders

One of the reasons Level 4 Leaders are able to develop other leaders is that the vision is big enough for all of them. Level 4 Leaders know that the best talent is attracted not solely by high-dollar offers, perks and power, or privilege, but also by a compelling vision. Level 4 Leaders don't mind surrounding themselves with talent and helping to grow that talent because they know there is enough to do for everybody. The accomplishment of the vision has taken priority over smaller, individual goals, which seem petty in comparison to the vision.

Level 4 Leaders know that the best talent is attracted not solely by high-dollar offers, perks and power, or privilege, but also by a
_____ _____.

Level 4 Leaders Know That Recognition Is the Most Valuable Motivator

At the Fourth Level of Influence, the leader is widely recognized as an expert in his or her field. Level 4 Leaders take some of the "spotlight" shining upon them and share it among the Performers on their team. They do this loudly and publicly, edifying and recognizing the stars in their organization.

Level 4 Leaders know that the real reason most people in their organization perform is for the very recognition and praise the Level 4 Leader bestows upon them. Where Level 3 Leaders are happy to receive praise and recognition for their own leadership performance, Level 4 Leaders know that they are not in competition with any of their people and share credit and praise in order to build and develop their leaders.

Some Level 3 Leaders actually become upset when their own people start matching their performance. Level 4 Leaders never behave that way; instead, they get out the checkered flag and wave their people past. That is the significant difference between simply *being* a leader oneself and *developing others* into leaders. Level 4 Leaders know the power of recognizing their leaders. They understand how critical it is in the development of others.

As the saying goes concerning recognition, "Babies cry for it, and grown men die for it." Level 4 Leaders require neither tears nor death before praising their leaders; they know to offer it lavishly.

Recognition: "Babies _____ for it, and grown men _____ for it."

Why is it important for a Level 4 Leader to share the credit as much as possible?

_____

_____

_____

Why is it hard for some to maintain a good attitude when their own people match or pass their performance?

_____

_____

_____

Actions or the "Science" of Leadership Development

At the Fourth Level of Influence, the "art" side of leadership is starting to outweigh the "science" side. However, this Fourth Level still embodies some very key steps.

Level 4 Leaders Compel Other Leaders to Get Team Results

At the previous Level of Influence, Level 3, the Leader was responsible for compelling people to *action*. The Level 4 Leader must compel people to obtain *results*. There is a big difference between getting people busy and making them effective. There is a time and place for activity as a focus, usually in the early days of a leader's experience. Activity breeds ability, confidence, and experience. But sooner or later, results are the name of the game. At Level 4, a leader's credibility comes from the results he is able to help *other* leaders attain.

The Level 4 Leader must compel people to obtain
_____.

What are the differences between a Level 3 Leader compelling people to action and a Level 4 Leader compelling people to obtain results?

_____

_____

_____

Level 4 Leaders Become Talent Scouts

Whenever an organization has effective Level 3 Leaders, it is a good bet that someone mentored and developed them. That is the job of a Level 4 Leader. This requires the Level 4 Leader to recognize potential leadership talent. John Maxwell writes in *Equipping 101*, "Great leaders seek out and find potential leaders, then transform them into good leaders."

For the purpose of this workbook, the focus will be on a few key areas that have been found to be the most important when attempting to identify leaders worthy of mentoring and developing. This list starts with the three Foundational Qualities of Leadership with which we began:

1. Hungry
2. Hone-able
3. Honorable

These three are required, but when identifying potential leaders, there are a few more attributes to consider so that the Level 4 Leader does not waste time mentoring those who will not blossom into effective leaders. These are

4. Activity
5. Respect
6. Connected relationship
7. Attitude
8. Relatability

"Great leaders seek out and find _____ leaders, then transform them into good leaders."

Why must a mentor look for certain attributes when deciding whom to mentor?

_____

_____

_____

ACTIVITY

Activity is a highly important attribute to look for in those who can potentially be developed into leaders because this is a strong indicator of ambition, courage, and initiative. It also becomes a differentiator that the mentor can use to explain the privilege of becoming a protégé. The mentor, or Level 4 Leader, might say to the protégé, "The reason I have you here instead of a thousand other candidates is because you've convinced me through your efforts that you want to become a leader. If you will do what it takes and follow my counsel, I'll teach you what you need to succeed."

When searching for potential leaders to develop, look for those with high levels of consistent activity, people who continually rotate through the Cycle of Achievement discussed earlier. It is impossible to steer a parked car, but a car in motion turns with ease. When it comes to finding potential leaders, look for someone in motion. Nearly everything else can be taught along the way.

It is impossible to _____ a parked car, but a car in _____ turns with ease.

Why is it important for a mentor to look for activity in a protégé?

_____

_____

_____

What kinds of activity matter the most?

_____

_____

_____

RESPECT

If a candidate for leadership development does not respect the Level 4 Leader, her accomplishments, and her counsel, the process breaks down before it begins. There must be belief that the mentor can provide what the protégé needs to succeed as a leader.

Respect breeds communication and cooperation and allows the successful sharing of power.

Why is it important for a mentor to look for respect in a protégé?

_____

_____

_____

What might happen if a protégé doesn't respect the mentor?

_____

_____

_____

CONNECTED RELATIONSHIP

This term represents a relationship where the mentor and the protégé just seem to "connect." For teaching and learning, the most productive arrangement is a relationship where both sides genuinely like each other.

Why is it important for the mentor and protégé to have a connected relationship?

_____

_____

_____

How can a mentor know if he or she connects with the protégé?

_____

_____

_____

What can the mentor do to increase the connection of the relationship?

_____

_____

_____

ATTITUDE

It is impossible to teach leadership without continually returning to the topic of attitude. Winners don't have better circumstances; they have better attitudes about their circumstances. Mentors should look closely for a positive attitude on the part of any candidate for leadership development. Without a proper attitude, there can be no personal growth.

Why is it important for a mentor to look for a proper attitude in a protégé?

_____

_____

_____

How can attitude affect the mentoring process?

_____

_____

_____

RELATABILITY

Leaders are in the business of influencing *people*. For that reason, any candidate for the leadership-development process must have a basic ability with people. We call this "relatability." A relatable person is liked, trusted, and listened to. They make a good first impression and an even better impression as the relationship deepens. They exude credibility. Mentors looking for a potential leader to groom would be well advised to choose candidates who already have a high degree of this ability with people.

Why is it important for a mentor to observe a protégé's relatability?

_____

_____

_____

Level 4 Leaders Empower Other Leaders

At Level 4, leaders are not just developing *followers*, they are developing *leaders*. There is a big difference between the two.

Empowering leaders involves giving them control and decision-making authority. It means letting them lead their own teams and make their own mistakes and, quite simply, giving them the freedom to fail or fly. True leaders will not stick with the Level 4 Leader unless given a chance to spread their wings and show what they can do because without that chance, they will never reach their potential. This is why it is said that average leaders lead followers while great leaders lead leaders.

Empowering leaders involves giving them _____ and _____ -_____ authority.

This week, find a situation in which you can empower someone else to do what you normally do. It could be letting your child plan a family event for the weekend or giving someone on your team authority over a project or activity. Answer the following questions throughout the week and evaluate the experience.

I helped empower:

_____

by letting him or her:

_____

_____

Why did you choose this person?

_____

_____

_____

What were your initial concerns?

_____

_____

_____

How did this person react to your offer?

_____

_____

_____

What were some of the challenges this person faced with the project, task, or decision?

_____

_____

_____

How did you encourage this person?

_____

_____

_____

How did you help the individual in your role as a leader?

_____

_____

_____

What was the outcome of the project, task, or decision?

_____

_____

_____

Was empowering this individual beneficial to you and that person? Explain.

_____

_____

Level 4 Leaders Learn to Mentor

The next most important skill for a Level 4 Leader to develop is the ability to mentor. The Level 3 Leader is a protégé to a mentor. At Level 4, he or she mentors others. Mentoring is an involved process that requires time, energy, discretion, patience, and discipline, and it can be difficult to carry out. But here lies the secret to multiplication within an organization and the secret to sustainable, continual growth of an organization's performance.

Mentoring and developing other leaders may seem like a lost art in today's "me first" society. Many "leaders" are wary of developing others to become peak performers out of fear of losing their own cushy leadership positions. Allow us to give a caution: Leaders who become wrapped up in themselves and seek only their own success and aggrandizement rarely last for long in the field of leadership. True leaders are secure in their ability to perform and know that the only way to maximize themselves as leaders is to *develop other leaders.* There is a true win-win situation when a leader mentors and grows another leader. And without bringing others along, the leader has reached a plateau.

True leaders are secure in their ability to _____ and know that the only way to maximize themselves as leaders is to _____ other leaders.

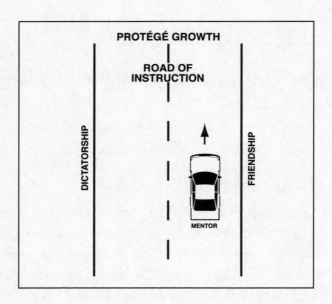

Level 4 Leaders must understand that the process of mentoring is a balancing act. Just as the road to success is bordered by Ditches of Discouragement and Complacency, the process of mentoring is bordered by the Ditches of Friendship and Dictatorship.

A mentor must stay just to the right of center. If a mentor becomes too much of a friend, the familiarity erodes respect and accountability on the part of the protégé in the relationship. If a mentor drifts toward becoming a dictator, the protégé will feel resentful and hurt; he'll lose motivation and eventually respect for the mentor. A mentor is someone who cares about the performance of the protégé enough to say what a friend would not. In this regard, a mentor actually goes *beyond* friendship. But a mentor also respects the protégé too much to ever become bossy or demanding.

Mentors should never assume that each of their trainees should be treated in the same manner. People are different, and they require differing treatment. We don't mean to imply *unequal* treatment, but *unique* treatment.

There are three main areas to identify when beginning to mentor someone. First is his or her personality or natural temperament. Second is his or her learning style. Some people learn best through visual instruction, others learn verbally, and still others learn best experientially. Third is his or her "love language." This involves the style of communication that a person prefers, such as verbal, touch, receiving gifts, quality time, and acts of service. Knowing these natural bents allows a mentor to provide spot-on instruction specifically tailored to the maximum impact on the individual being developed.

A mentor is someone who cares about the _____
of the protégé enough to say what a _____
would not.

Mentors should never assume that each of their trainees should be treated in the _____ manner.

There are _____ main areas to identify when beginning to mentor someone.

Write down the names of three mentors you have had in your life, and next to the names, list abilities that they helped you develop.

	Mentor	Abilities
1.	_____	_____
2.	_____	_____
3.	_____	_____

Who has been your most effective mentor? Describe your relationship with the person.

_____

_____

_____

Why was this mentor so effective with you?

_____

_____

_____

Did you enjoy being around this leader? Why or why not?

_____

_____

_____

How did this person inspire you to work harder to achieve certain goals?

_____

_____

_____

Mentoring involves many steps. Much of it is more art than science. In fact, mentoring can be looked upon as long-term brain surgery. The overall intent is to teach the protégé how to think correctly as a leader. Ninety-five percent of mentoring is about helping the protégé develop proper thinking. In this section, we will break the process down into its component parts to reveal the art and teach the science.

SETS THE EXAMPLE

Example is an important part in all leadership functions, but especially in mentorship. Followers need help. Leaders need an example. The mentor must have fruit on the tree to be an effective counselor because to know and not to have is not to know.

To know and not to _____ is not to _____.

ASKS QUESTIONS

At first, the mentor simply has to get to know the protégé because we cannot lead those we do not know. Regarding the protégé, the mentor wishes to know:

1. What makes him tick?
2. What makes him special?
3. Why did he get involved in his particular field?
4. What motivates him? What are his dreams?
5. What is his personality or temperament?
6. What challenges has he had in his life?
7. What victories has he had?
8. What principles does he understand and embody?
9. What principles does he still need to learn?
10. What blind spots does he have about himself?
11. What is his commitment level?

12. What is the basis of his character?
13. Where is his thinking?

The key for a mentor is to be a good listener. A good mentor asks and listens and observes, taking mental notes, digging deeper into issues that are especially illuminating into the thinking of the protégé. Listening will tell the mentor where the protégé's thinking is and how he interprets information, what his perspective is, and how ambitious he really is for his goals.

We cannot lead those we do not _____.

The key for a mentor is to be a good _____.

BUILDS THE RELATIONSHIP

For the leadership-development process to be effective, the protégé must have 100 percent trust that what the mentor is telling him is in his best interest. Webster defines trust as the "assured reliance on the character, ability, strength, or truth of someone or something." This level of reliance can occur only where there is relationship.

Mentors must seek to bond with their protégés, and there are no shortcuts when it comes to relationships. The mentor must invest time on a regular basis in building and securing the relationship. This is especially important when it becomes time for the mentor to provide course correction or address issues of deficiency head-on. At that time, there had better be a relationship the mentor can draw upon. John Maxwell wrote, "Never underestimate the power of building relationships with people before asking them to follow you."

Why is trust such an important part of the relationship between the mentor and the protégé?

_____

_____

_____

Give an example of a time when a leader violated your trust. What was your reaction?

_____

_____

_____

After someone violates your trust, how is it regained?

_____

_____

_____

Can you think of instances in which you have violated followers' trust? If so, how did/will you work to restore it?

_____

_____

_____

How effective will a leader be if he or she has lost the trust of the team?

_____

_____

_____

What is the quickest way for a person to lose your trust?

_____

_____

_____

How do you gain and maintain the trust of others?

_____

_____

_____

AFFIRMS THE PROTÉGÉ

Everyone needs to be accepted, and leaders are no different. Mentors affirm their protégés by accepting them as a person of value and someone worthy of respect. The newer the relationship, the more important it is that the mentor remain nonjudgmental. There will be plenty of time throughout the leadership-development process to make adjustments and inspire personal growth. However, the doorway to positive change will never be opened unless the protégé is first accepted and affirmed for who he is at the outset.

Everyone needs to be _____, and leaders are no different.

The newer the relationship, the more important it is that the mentor remain _____.

Why is it important for the mentor to affirm the protégé?

_____

_____

_____

BUILDS THE PROTÉGÉ'S BELIEF

It is very difficult to accomplish anything unless there is belief in the objective, the plan, the leadership, and the cause behind it all. On an even deeper level, it is very difficult to accomplish anything when a person doesn't have belief in his or her own ability. Mentors stand by with evidences of past performance and reassurances from the well of their own experience to bolster the protégé's belief in him- or herself and the possibility of achievement. Anthony Robbins explains that beliefs must be supported by upholding evidences, much as a stool must be upheld by its legs. The upholding legs of belief are comprised of:

1. evidence of past performance
2. character
3. values

Mentors help bolster the belief a protégé has in herself by reminding her of these supporting evidences.

Why is it important for the mentor to build the protégé's belief?

_____

_____

_____

BUILDS THE PROTÉGÉ'S DREAM

Another key component of a mentor's responsibilities is to help the protégé develop his dream. Mentors have walked and seen farther, and they can help the protégé dream and think bigger than he could on his own. Many times, leaders cannot see how far their own greatness will carry them, but a mentor can. As John Wanamaker observes, "A man is not doing much until the cause he works for possesses all there is of him."

Many times, leaders cannot see how far their own _____ will carry them, but a mentor can.

Why is it important for the mentor to build the protégé's dream?

_____

_____

_____

What are some ways a mentor can help build a protégé's dream?

_____

_____

_____

KILLS THE PROTÉGÉ'S FEAR

Fear is the show-stopper that arrests the development of a leader at the edge of her comfort zone. Mentors provide the jailbreak. This can be done through reframing situations to help protégés see things in a different light. It may be done by exposing the issues causing anxiety for the wafer-thin obstacles they really are. Usually, it involves the mentor encouraging the protégé to confront her fears head-on. Just pushing through these barriers is a fear-killer, and mentors are there to provide that push with courage on loan. Courage is not action without fear but action in spite of fear. Mentors foster that courage.

Courage is not action without _____ but action in _____ of fear.

GIVES CONFIDENCE

One way mentors engender courage in the hearts of their protégés is by building their confidence. Mentors help build and restore confidence by pointing out past victories and reminding the leader of his strengths and abilities. A mentor builds confidence by being specific. Flattery and loose words mean nothing and may actually serve to diminish a leader's confidence even further. "Remember that time you overcame X problem? How did you do that? Well, you'll do this the same way, and you're a much stronger leader now than you were then."

A mentor builds confidence by being _____.

KEEPS THE PROTÉGÉ IN THE ACTION PHASE

Another way mentors build confidence is by keeping their protégés in the game. Confidence in performance usually slackens when the leader's activity level drops. Remembering past victories and performances goes only so far. There is nothing like new success to bolster confidence, and mentors take advantage of this truth. Keeping their protégés in the game is half the battle of building confidence.

The action phase is also required for the development of proper habits. When leaders develop good habits, their capability becomes an unconscious competence; they can perform well without having to stop and think too much about it. Often a leader has little time to make key decisions. The ability to make correct decisions in the heat of battle can be developed only by living in the action phase long enough to gain effective habits and have good judgment become part of one's instincts. None of this can be learned anywhere else except in the action phase.

Keeping their protégés in the game is half the battle of building
_____.

The action phase is also required for the development of proper
_____.

Why is staying in the action phase important?

_____

_____

_____

REFRAMES THE PROTÉGÉ'S CHALLENGES

Mentors can provide perspective on the challenges facing a leader. This is done through reframing, where the mentor takes the challenge as defined by the protégé and "reframes" it in a different light. The protégé may see only lemons, but the mentor shows how to make them into lemonade. It is nothing more than presenting the evidence in a way that convinces the leader that she can still have success. Without proper reframing, obstacles can look insurmountable. It's not what happens, but how the leader sees what happens, that counts. Mentors help their leaders see things in the proper way.

The protégé may see only _____, but the mentor shows how to make them into _____.

It's not what _____, but how the leader _____ what happens, that counts.

Why is it important for the mentor to help reframe the protégé's challenges?

_____

_____

_____

ALLOWS STRUGGLE TO INSTRUCT

While it is important to reframe challenges and obstacles in the proper perspective as we have just discussed, it is also the job of the mentor to allow struggles to impart their wisdom. It is rightly said that we learn more from our mistakes than any of our successes. In the case of any great leader, it was the struggles that made him great.

Level 4 Leaders know that their protégés will be refined in the fiery furnace of struggle, and they allow it and help impart the lessons being learned along the way. As mentors, Level 4 Leaders must help their protégés realize that the breakfast of champions is not cereal, but struggle. After all, struggle is the seasoning that makes victory taste sweet.

In the case of any great leader, it was the _____
that made him great.

Why must the mentor allow the protégé to struggle?

_____

_____

_____

What lessons have you learned from past struggles?

_____

_____

_____

Encourages the Protégé

On the heels of reframing comes encouragement. Every leader needs encouragement. Mentors let protégés know that they have the seeds of greatness deep inside, that they do have what it takes to make it.

Every leader needs _____.

Spreads Contagious Enthusiasm

Ralph Waldo Emerson said, "Nothing great was ever achieved without enthusiasm." Walter Chrysler tells us, "The real secret of success is enthusiasm. Yes, more than enthusiasm I would say excitement. I like to see men get excited. When they get excited, they make a success of their lives." Enthusiasm is contagious, like a fire in dry wood, spreading from place to place. Mentors are fire starters and stokers, keeping the flames of excitement in their protégés burning bright. Enthusiasm is a feeling, and mentors must become adept at transferring that feeling.

Enthusiasm is _____, like a fire in dry wood, spreading from place to place.

Why is enthusiasm so contagious?

_____

_____

_____

TEACHES THE PHILOSOPHY

All effective organizations and their leaders have a philosophy of success, a roadmap of behavior and thinking that explains and continues their history of accomplishment. It is the job of a Level 4 Leader to inculcate that philosophy into the hearts and minds of the leaders being developed. Every interaction between the mentor and his protégé is an opportunity to preach and teach the winning philosophy.

It is the job of a Level 4 Leader to inculcate that _____ into the hearts and minds of the _____ being developed.

Whose winning philosophy are you following?

_____

_____

_____

Why is it important for a mentor to have a set philosophy of success?

_____

_____

_____

IMPARTS HIS OR HER THINKING (COMMON SENSE)

One of the most important objectives for a mentor is to gradually impart his entire way of thinking into the protégé. This is not an easy or a fast process. It can result only as a product of time spent together addressing issues in a constructive way. It requires diligent study on the part of the protégé and careful questioning and instruction from the mentor. As time goes on, the protégé should react to new circumstances with a question: What would my mentor think about this? Eventually, in a well-developed relationship, the protégé will take challenges to the mentor with a best-guess analysis of what the mentor will most likely say and recommend. In this way, the protégé can embody the thinking and learn to apply it to whatever comes along.

As time goes on, the protégé should react to new _____ with a question: What would my _____ think about this?

Why is it important for the mentor to impart his or her thinking into the protégé?

_____

_____

_____

COURSE-CORRECTS AND CONFRONTS THE ISSUES

We discussed this concept of course correction in the Cycle of Achievement when we stressed the importance of seeking counsel. This is a very big area of operation for a Level 4 Leader. When mentoring, it's a leader's job to identify where the protégé is off track and provide correction to get him back on track.

1. What principles is the protégé missing?
2. What are her thinking patterns and how are they wrong?
3. How is his perspective in need of reframing?
4. How can the protégé see things differently so that she behaves or performs more effectively?
5. How are his attitudes inappropriate or unproductive?
6. What does the protégé need to see that she doesn't see, and how can the mentor help her see it?

These are the types of questions a mentor explores when listening to the protégé and probing for a correct view of the situation. This is necessary because all of us have "blind spots" in our lives. There are problems or weaknesses that we just cannot see ourselves (though others may). Mentors will notice that their protégés are both "willfully blind" and "blindly willful" when it comes to these blind spots, and it is the mentor's job to help the protégé confront these areas.

Course correction must be done in love. Remember, the protégé must first know beyond a doubt that the mentor has his best interests at heart. Only upon this platform can effective course correction be provided. The terminology we like comes from Josh McDowell and Bob Hostetler in their excellent book *The New Tolerance*. McDowell and Hostetler say that we must speak with "humble truth and aggressive love." Humble truth says that course correction occurs gently and in kindness so that the protégé does not become demoralized. Aggressive love says that the feeling of care and respect is so strong that the mentor is free to administer correction without hurting the feelings or pride of the protégé.

This process of confronting issues requires close observation and listening, but it also demands tact. Mentors must learn to use "velvet sledgehammers" when removing flies from the foreheads of their protégés. Issues must be addressed, and the best method is to attack them when issues are still small. Recall that it's easier to pluck out a tiny twig now than cut down a large oak later.

One of the best techniques for addressing areas of concern with protégés is the "sandwich method." This involves complimenting the student leader on areas of strength and on specific noteworthy accomplishments. Next, the mentor addresses the problem with warmth and understanding, but nonetheless boldly. The mentor's objective should be to "get it all out on the table." Finally, once the issues have been directly confronted and discussed to their productive conclusion (protégé acknowledgment, commitment to improve or correct the issue, and all questions answered), the mentor can then exit the discussion by building up the trainee again, reminding the trainee about his or her opportunities and emphasizing that it has been the behavior and not the person that has been corrected. Remember, it is vital that the protégé understand how much the mentor cares. It would certainly be easier for the mentor to ignore uncomfortable conversations (at least in the moment), but the mentor addresses these things because he or she cares about the student.

We must speak with "_____ truth and _____ love."

Mentors must learn to use "_____ sledgehammers" when removing flies from the foreheads of their protégés.

One of the best techniques for addressing areas of concern with protégés is the "_____ method."

When is the best time for the mentor to course-correct? Why?

_____

_____

_____

Why is it important how the mentor course-corrects?

_____

_____

_____

What might happen if the mentor uses aggressive truth and humble love instead of humble truth and aggressive love?

_____

_____

_____

Gets the Protégé to Take Responsibility

A very large part of mentoring involves the concept of taking responsibility. It is a natural tendency for each of us to search for excuses or alibis when things don't go our way. Leaders do not have this luxury. Mentors must train their protégés in the art of taking responsibility not only for their actions, but also for their results.

The attitude of a mentor should be "I won't take the credit when you win. I won't take the blame when you don't." Earlier, when we talked about accepting the blame and sharing the credit, we were discussing a leader's general position at the helm of a team. In the mentoring process, however, the mentor passes the accountability to the protégé. It is as if the baton of leadership is being passed. Now it is the protégé's war, and the mentor is teaching him to lead it.

Remember, the mentor already has fruit on the tree to demonstrate that his information has value. The protégé must then take that information and assume responsibility for its implementation and the results of that implementation.

"I won't take the _____ when you win. I won't take the _____ when you don't."

Why is it important that the mentor gets the protégé to take responsibility?

_____

_____

_____

HOLDS THE PROTÉGÉ ACCOUNTABLE

Leaders are accountable for their own actions—period. It is the job of the mentor to teach this habit. It begins when the mentor holds the developing leader accountable for his results, and "forces" him to measure up to his true potential. This works because people will often do for the approval of someone else what they won't accomplish for themselves. A relationship is cultivated in which the protégé wants to perform to earn the respect of the mentor. In fact, earning respect is a prerequisite to continuing the training. If a mentor is giving time and energy to the development of a future leader and nothing is changing or improving (measurable improvement in a reasonable amount of time), then the mentor is wasting time and should find a more worthy student.

A relationship is _____ in which the protégé wants to perform to earn the _____ of the mentor.

Why is holding the protégé accountable important in the mentoring process?

_____

_____

_____

What are some ways the protégé can stay accountable to the mentor?

_____

_____

_____

CHALLENGES THE PROGÉGÉ

Hunger and *desire* are key to the ongoing development of a protégé. This springs largely from the challenge a leader feels to perform; and for high achievers, the greater the challenge, the greater the performance. When Michael Jordan retired the first time from basketball and decided to play baseball instead, it was because he felt he had run out of challenges on the basketball court. Mentors make sure their developing leaders remain challenged. Questions a Level 4 Leader or mentor might ask to be sure the protégé is challenged are:

1. What vision are you currently pursuing?
2. What goals do you have to fulfill that vision?
3. What type of activity would be required to accomplish that?
4. Are you willing to do the work?
5. How strong is your commitment?
6. What type of person would be required to accomplish that?
7. Are you willing to change to become that person?

Keeping leaders challenged fuels their growth and gives them the power to improve their way upward through increasing Levels of Influence.

What might happen if the protégé does not feel challenged?

_____

_____

_____

PURSUES A HEART CHANGE

All these steps in mentoring are fine, but they will add up to nothing if they somehow bypass the heart. In *Instruments in the Redeemer's Hands*, Paul David Tripp writes, "If the heart doesn't change, the person's words and behavior may change temporarily because of an external pressure or incentive. But when the pressure or incentive is removed, the changes will disappear. The body always goes where the heart leads."

Too many times, people make changes on the outside but become discouraged when the results don't last. That is because they have not committed to change way down deep, at the level of the heart. Mentors pursue change and growth in the heart of their protégés because that is the only place where change lasts. The results come later and are obvious and sustained.

"The _____ always goes where the _____ leads."

Why is it important for the protégé to pursue a heart change?

_____

_____

_____

What are some ways you can tell if someone has truly had a heart change and not just a change of some technique?

_____

_____

_____

Do you know of any example of someone who truly had a change of heart? If so, explain the noticeable differences. Did the changes last?

_____

_____

_____

Develops Balance in the Protégé

It may be helpful at this point to share the five categories or areas of personal growth that may be used throughout the course of developing a leader. These categories are:

1. Finances
2. Faith
3. Family
4. Friends
5. Fitness

These five areas can be compared to the spokes of a wagon wheel. Any spoke out of balance with the others drastically affects the operation of the wheel. A person's wellness in one area affects the others. It only stands to reason that growth in all the categories helps in the life of the protégé across the board. Conversely, poor performance in one or two areas will affect the other categories in a negative sense. And for some reason, the negative seems to be many times more capable of spreading across the categories than the positive. Over time, one of the objectives of the leadership-development process is to enhance each of the categories and eventually arrive at a balance or harmony among them.

Finances are first. This is because the mentoring process usually starts in a career setting, which has a direct impact on finances. But the disciplines that are required not only to earn more money, but to save, budget, and invest, are extremely valuable to building confidence and stability. Finances are also very measurable and underscore the ability of the mentor to help the protégé succeed.

Faith is really the most important. After all, submitting to God and fulfilling His purpose in life is ultimately what life is all about. Further, strong faith in a calling and purpose is essential for significance as a leader. However, it may take a while before a protégé feels comfortable enough with a mentor to open up in this area. Nonetheless, this area must be addressed as a major focal point for ongoing growth.

Family is critical also. It really doesn't matter how successful a leader becomes if he doesn't have his private life put together. Strife at home in the most personal, private relationships we have is poison to our well-being, happiness, and productivity. Mentors will not omit this area if they truly want to help developing leaders achieve complete success.

Friends are a crucial consideration in the growth of a leader. This is because for so many people, the crowd they associate with is not productive in their life. Many times, people who strongly desire to change and grow, who even begin making some of the tough decisions and steps in that direction, continue associating with their old friends and acquaintances. At worst, these associations are destructive to their personal growth and often blow them from the path of success altogether. At best, these relationships add little value. Mentors know up-and-coming leaders must choose their association with others wisely.

Fitness makes the list, of course, because none of the successes or responsibilities of a leader mean anything if the leader is in poor health. Not only do proper diet and exercise help the leader live longer to enjoy the fruits of his labor and maximize his contributions to the world, but they also make him more energized and effective in his daily living.

It is understandable that keeping the five spokes of the wheel exactly in balance is unrealistic, but as Vince Lombardi said, "We are going to give perfection one [heck] of a chase, and if we never get it, we'll certainly catch excellence along the way!" Spoken like a true mentor!

It only stands to reason that _____ in all the _____ helps in the life of the protégé across the board.

It really doesn't matter how _____ a leader becomes if he doesn't have his private_____ put together.

Why is it important for the protégé to work toward a balanced life?

_____

_____

_____

What might happen if the protégé is not mentored in one or more of these categories?

_____

_____

_____

If the mentor is not an expert in one of these categories, how can he or she still help the protégé in that area?

_____

_____

_____

Developing Leaders: Lord Horatio Nelson — "Every Captain Was a Nelson"

The Battle of Trafalgar was really the zenith of the fascinating age of fighting sail. There Admiral Viscount Lord Horatio Nelson completed one of his most astonishing annihilations of his French and Spanish adversaries and was killed in the process.

What we wrote in the original *Launching a Leadership Revolution* book about Nelson's victory at the Battle of the Nile a few years earlier was also true of his conduct at Trafalgar. Nelson spent considerable time developing his ship's captains. He met with them every chance he got to impart his fighting philosophy to them. He held special dinners to get them acquainted with each other to foster better teamwork. And most important, when the battle commenced, he turned them loose to fight on their own. Since the battle was confusing and communication across the smoky water was extremely difficult, with the loud cannons roaring almost nonstop, trying to coordinate fleet movements was nearly impossible anyway. Nelson's preference was to rely on the ability of his fighting captains to make their own decisions in the heat of battle and to act on the philosophy he had painstakingly taught them beforehand. As his fleet sailed into battle, Nelson's flagship made a few signals to coordinate the fleet's movements as it came into battle. But once the fighting began, Nelson's signals changed to those of encouragement to "engage the enemy more closely" and, famously, "England expects every man will do his duty."

This style of fighting, a significant departure from the standard method of engagement in the Royal Navy at that time, was what Nelson called the "Nelson touch." Uniquely, Nelson was the only fleet commander in British history that purposely brought on a "pell-mell" battle and succeeded at it time and again. The reasons were many. But primary among them was the fighting initiative of his individual captains. They clearly knew what Nelson expected of them, and they performed accordingly. Nelson had the master touch of decentralizing his leadership style at the right moment to wreak the greatest possible destruction on his enemy.

Perhaps no one summed up the results of the "Nelson touch" quite as well as Vice-Admiral Villeneuve, the French fleet commander who was defeated at Trafalgar. He was said to have made the following comment after learning of Lord Nelson's death at the battle: "To any other Nation the loss of a Nelson would have been irreparable, but in the British Fleet off Cadiz, every Captain was a Nelson." The Battle of Trafalgar is a prime example of the power of the Fourth Level of Influence.

Nelson and his captains had done it. Such a victory could not have been obtained by one man. Nor could it have been accomplished by leadership practices of a lower level than those employed. *(Without developing other leaders, one is limited to the performance of only followers.)* The victory required the coordinated effort of many leaders. Although the British government had received tremendous criticism for entrusting the operation to so young a commander, Nelson had demonstrated his ability not only as a seaman, but also as a *leader of other leaders*. Napoleon himself would later say, "If it had not been for you English, I should have been emperor of the East; but wherever there is water to float a ship, we are to find you in our way." This was due in large part to the legacy begun by Nelson and his captains, which continued through the remainder of the century. *(Level 4 Leaders leave a legacy through the leaders they develop.)*

Nelson was a true Level 4 Leader. He had *found* and *developed* other leaders capable of performing at the levels he himself had earlier in his illustrious career, thereby significantly expanding his influence. *(A Level 4 Leader is only as good as the leaders he develops.)* He took them under his wing, giving careful instruction, teaching them his fighting philosophy and his way of thinking, and empowering them with the responsibility for results when it mattered most *(Level 4 Leaders empower other leaders to lead their own teams, giving them the freedom to succeed as leaders in their own right).*

Nelson had crafted the most effective fighting squadron the world's oceans had ever witnessed. When the moment of truth came, the hours of careful investment in developing other leaders paid off.

How were the captains able to coordinate and continue fighting after their leader, Lord Nelson, died during battle?

_____

_____

_____

If Lord Nelson had not properly trained his captains to be able to fight both on their own and together, what might have happened when he was killed during the battle?

_____

_____

_____

Have you been involved in an organization where the leader left and the progress of the organization continued to grow? If so, explain what happened.

_____

_____

_____

Have you been involved in an organization where the leader left and the progress of the organization diminished? If so, explain what happened.

_____

_____

_____

Summary

We close this instruction on Level 4 Leadership with a short summary, paraphrased from Paul David Tripp. Level 4 Leaders:

1. Love people
2. Know people
3. Speak truth into their lives
4. Help them lead where God has called them to lead

CHAPTER 10

The Fifth Level of Influence: Developing Leaders Who Develop Leaders

Really great men have a curious feeling that the greatness is not in them, but through them.

—JOHN RUSKIN

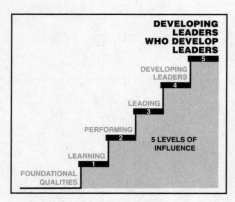

The Fifth Level of Influence is the pinnacle of leadership ability. Whereas the influence of Level 3 Leaders lasts as long as the leader does and Level 4 Influence lasts as long as the leader's leaders are around, Level 5 Influence outlasts everybody. Level 5 Influence is seen on those rare occasions when a leader not only becomes very accomplished as a leader himself and not only succeeds at developing other leaders, but also manages to develop leaders who can then develop other leaders who continue the legacy onward. In history, Level 5 Influence has defined movements and ideas that echoed down through generations, profoundly impacting the world.

Our example of the soccer player gets stretched by the time Level 5 Influence is considered. Nevertheless, it is conceivable that the athlete not only matured into a great leader and coach, but became legendary as well. Perhaps she pioneered new techniques or training methods and revolutionized the entire sport. Her following among the world's soccer players became enormous, as those she developed in turn developed others. There would most likely be innovations named after her or perhaps even a professional team. At this point, her influence would have reached Level 5.

Why would someone want to strive to become a Level 5 Leader?

_____

_____

_____

What is a major difference in the results of a Level 5 Leader compared with those of a Level 4 Leader?

_____

_____

_____

Presuppositions or the "Art" of Level 5

Level 5 Leaders understand:

1. Results will come through the endurance and succession of the vision.
2. The vision and the leader are intertwined.

Results Will Come through the Endurance and Succession of the Vision

A Level 5 Leader can be identified by the magnitude of the following he or she leaves behind. The size of the vision, its enduring legacy, and its successful continuation in the hands of other leaders is the fruit of a Level 5 Leader's efforts. Whereas Level 1 Leaders are only as good as what they learn, Level 2 Leaders are only as good as their personal performance, Level 3 Leaders are only as good as the performance of their team, and Level 4 Leaders are only as good as the performance of their leaders, Level 5 Leaders are only as good as the enduring quality and succession of their vision.

The size of the _____, its enduring _____, and its successful continuation in the hands of other leaders is the fruit of a Level 5 Leader's efforts.

The Vision and the Leader Are Intertwined

A Level 5 Leader is not only clear about the vision and not even just capable of casting it before the organization, but he or she actually comes to embody that very vision. One cannot think of Martin Luther King Jr. without thinking of the civil rights movement and his "I have a dream" vision for an America built on true equality of opportunity. The memory still rings sweet generations later. His leadership attracted thousands of America's best and brightest leaders to a cause that burned in their hearts, produced changes in the laws of the United States, and taught leaders elsewhere how to protest peacefully, honorably, and successfully. His vision and example inspired later leaders and movements such as Nelson Mandela and the end of apartheid in South Africa and Lech Walesa and the movement to free Poland from Soviet Communism. As King himself said, "If a man hasn't found something he is willing to die for, he isn't fit to live."

Level 5 Leaders get so wrapped up in their cause that they come to embody that very cause. The leader is almost lost inside the vision.

A Level 5 Leader is not only clear about the _____ and not even just capable of _____ it before the organization, but he or she actually comes to _____ that very vision.

Why are the vision and a Level 5 Leader intertwined together?

_____

_____

_____

Can you think of another example of a leader who embodies his or her vision?

_____

_____

_____

Actions or the "Science" of Level 5

At Level 5 Leadership, there is not much science left; almost everything has become art. At Level 5, it's who the leader is and what he or she stands for more than what the leader does that makes the impact. This is one reason Level 5 Leaders are so rare.

Please don't misunderstand us here. Level 5 Leaders have been "doing" for a long time, probably their whole adult lives, in order to reach this pinnacle of leadership impact. Their example has resonated and created a following of the highest caliber of leaders. Their very being has seemingly metastasized into the vision

itself. Level 5 Leaders have decreased themselves, many times sac-
rificially, in order to increase the vision. As John the Baptist said
when Jesus began His ministry, "I must decrease so that He can
increase." Level 5 Leaders embody a similar sentiment. They must
decrease in order for the cause to increase.

With all this said, the main action for Level 5 Leaders is: attracting and developing the highest-caliber leaders available for the
cause.

"I must _____ so that He can
_____."

Why is there not much more science to learn at Level 5?

_____

_____

_____

Why must a Level 5 Leader decrease him- or herself in order for
the cause to increase?

_____

_____

_____

What are some ways a Level 5 Leader might decrease him- or herself in order for the cause to increase?

_____

_____

_____

Attract the Highest-Caliber Leaders to the Cause

There comes a point in the development of other leaders where the mentor is limited by the attributes of the protégé. Becoming a Level 5 Leader requires followers who are at the Fourth Level of Influence, and many, many leaders will never even reach that height but will instead plateau at the Third Level. So Level 5 Influence hinges on the ability of the leader to find people of the highest caliber to develop and to retain them.

How are leaders of the highest caliber attracted in the first place? At this level of discussion, perks or incentives or great stock option plans will no longer do it. Top leadership talent is rarely attracted to such trinkets as a major point of focus. Instead, the top leaders in any field are attracted only by a strong and compelling vision, one they can believe in, one that provides room for them to make their mark, and one that speaks to their inner calling.

Finding Level 4 Leaders to develop requires a very mature, confident leader. At this Level of Influence, there is no room for ego or the petty jealousy of power that besets many leaders at the Fourth or even the Third Level of Influence. Level 5 Leadership requires that the leader surround himself with people of ability even higher than his own, which is opposite of human nature. Small leaders surround themselves with followers; big leaders surround themselves with other leaders. The biggest of all leaders, Level 5 Leaders, surround themselves with leaders who have the potential of eclipsing their own personal glory.

So to become a Level 5 Leader, one must have his ego solidly in check, but that is not all. Leading Level 4 Leaders is not easy. By definition, Level 4 Leaders are strong and think for themselves. They have their own ideas and stand up firmly for what they believe. Consensus will rarely be present, which Level 5 Leaders know is a preferred condition. So Level 5 Leaders must also be able to handle a bit of unrest as they let their Level 4 Leaders speak their minds and exercise decisions they think prudent.

Level 5 Influence hinges on the ability of the leader to find _____ of the highest caliber to _____, and to _____ them.

The biggest of all leaders, Level 5 Leaders, surround themselves with leaders who have the potential of _____ their own personal glory.

_____ will rarely be present, which Level 5 Leaders know is a preferred condition.

Can someone who is beyond excellent in all leadership areas be considered a Level 5 Leader if he or she is not mentoring any Level 4 Leaders? Explain.

_____

_____

_____

How can a Level 5 Leader attract leaders of the highest caliber?

_____

_____

_____

Why is it so important for a Level 5 Leader to have his ego in check?

_____

_____

_____

This brings us to the topic of "meddling" or, as modern management theorists say, "micromanagement." Former president Jimmy Carter had one of the most unsuccessful administrations in presidential history. It had nothing to do with his character, as he is regarded by most as a decent and thoroughly honest man. However, his influence was severely limited by his inability to delegate authority and his obsessive need to be involved in every little detail of his administration.

Perhaps the best contrast with Carter's style can be seen in his successor, Ronald Reagan. In *Ronald Reagan: How an Ordinary Man Became an Extraordinary Leader*, author Dinesh D'Souza describes a famous incident that occurred near the end of the Carter administration:

Reagan had just been elected, and Carter felt it was important to brief him on some of the major issues that the new president would have to face. Carter went down the list, discussing various treaties and secret agreements the United States had with other countries. Reagan listened politely but did not write anything down or ask any questions. "The information was 'quite complex,'" Carter writes, "and I did not see how he could possibly retain all of it merely by listening."

Carter felt that the details mattered and, thus, mastered them himself. Reagan left the details to his subordinates and focused on the big picture. The difference between the two presidents was more than just style; it was a difference in Leadership Level.

Level 5 Leaders must allow their Level 4 Leaders to *actually lead their leaders* and to live and learn from their own results. A leader who meddles will never attract or retain the highest leadership talent because true leaders refuse to be "governed"; they will only agree, at the most, to be "guided."

A leader who _____ will never attract or retain the highest leadership talent.

From the example above, in what way did Reagan's leadership level differ from Carter's?

_____

_____

_____

Why would micromanaging and "meddling" hinder the influence of a Level 5 Leader?

_____

_____

_____

How can a Level 5 Leader still get the little things done without micromanaging his other leaders?

_____

_____

_____

Developing Leaders Who Develop Leaders: The Apostle Paul—"An Influence of Inestimable Value"

He was a poor man, surviving on the generosity of his followers and his humble occupation of tent making. Conventional history has him small in stature, unimposing, and perhaps even slightly deformed. He was elected to no position, held no official authority, had no trappings of success. The man first known as Saul of Tarsus and later renamed Paul had none of the outward features the modern world thinks of when considering the term "leader," but he was, outside of Jesus, the greatest Level 5 Leader history has ever produced.

It was sometime around AD 64, and the setting was Rome, the very epicenter of the civilized world. Paul had been taken prisoner in Jerusalem and blamed with starting a riot in the temple there. He had been transported to Caesarea, a Roman city on the east coast of the Mediterranean Sea, to stand trial. He was tried by three separate Roman officials, who each to some extent were personally affected by his testimony, and was retained there for over two years. At some point in the proceedings, Paul invoked his rights as a Roman citizen, which necessitated his appearance in the capital city of Rome to stand further trial. A treacherous sea voyage resulted in a shipwreck on the shores of the island of Malta. That following spring, after the winter storms had subsided, Paul was finally taken to Rome to stand trial, quite possibly in front of the ruthless Emperor Nero himself. He would have to wait, though, and was placed under house arrest for another two years.

This grand imprisonment and adventure followed a life of hardships and persecution. In Paul's own words, "Of the Jews five times received I forty stripes [whippings] save one. Thrice was I beaten with rods, once was I stoned, thrice I suffered shipwreck, a night and a day I have been in the deep; In journeying often, in perils of waters, in perils of robbers, in perils by mine own countrymen, in perils by the heathen, in perils in the city, in perils in the wilderness, in perils in the sea, in perils among false brethren; In weariness and painfulness, in watching often, in hunger and thirst, in fastings often, in cold and nakedness" (2 Corinthians 11:24–27). He had traveled extensively, ignoring these perils to his person, pursuing one great, bold vision of spreading the news of Christ's death and resurrection to the world. All along the way he had taken companions. These men he taught and trained in the arts of leadership, teaching them about his great faith in Christ and the importance of their sacrifice as servant leaders to spread the word of the gospel throughout the then civilized world. He had "planted" churches in cities from Asia Minor to Macedonia, in the important city of Ephesus and the debauched city of Corinth, and in one of the ancient world's most advanced metropolises, the city of Antioch. Perhaps most remarkably, as a result of his long imprisonment there, an active, thriving church was begun right in Rome, the seat of the government of the empire and center of pagan religions.

Further, he created the opportunity to teach and debate the finest minds in the world in Athens, the centerpiece of intellectual thought and home of philosophy. At each location, he had schooled entire groups of leaders and followers to carry on the great work after he had moved on. He wrote profusely—instructing, teaching, rebuking, counseling, and coaching through letters that were delivered by his private couriers. According to Albert Barnes, author of *The Life of the Apostle Paul*, "No less than thirteen, and probably fourteen out of the twenty-seven books of the New Testament were written by him, or at his dictation." These writings served not only as continuing guidance to his leaders, who, at the time, were spread out around the Roman Empire, but became guideposts to millions of followers the world over, down through the next two millennia.

With all he had done, however, many look upon Paul's trial before the rulers of Rome as his high-water mark. According to author John MacArthur in *The Book on Leadership*, "That moment was, in effect, the pinnacle of Paul's ministry and the fulfillment of his deepest desire. He was called to be the apostle to the Gentiles. Rome was the cosmopolitan center of the pagan world. Paul had long sought an opportunity to preach the gospel in such a venue before the world's most important political leaders and philosophical trendsetters. This was that opportunity." Paul's vision had taken him into the very eye of the storm, where he courageously faced up to the duty of his calling.

By Paul's own account, after this "first trial" he was "delivered from the mouth of the lion" and set free. There are many conjectures about his further travels into Spain and again into Macedonia. Soon enough, most likely as part of the massive Christian persecution following the burning of Rome (started by Nero himself to clear the way for the building of a great temple and conveniently blamed on the Christians), Paul was again imprisoned in Rome. This time, however, there would be no amiable conditions of "house arrest." He was placed in a damp, dark hole in the ground, according to historical legend, in the base of the Mamertine Prison. Here he wrote his final letters while awaiting execution. At that point, Paul's whereabouts and activities vanish from the record. Most likely, he was beheaded just outside Rome on the Ostian Way.

The man had perished, but his work lived on. In the years following Paul's death, the churches he and his followers had started flourished and grew, reaching out around the countryside and starting other churches.

Paul had left behind a host of other leaders to carry on his vision. His main protégé, Timothy, was the recipient of two specific letters. Paul wrote these letters "in order to pass the mantle of church leadership to his young protégé," said John MacArthur. "He regarded Timothy as a clone of himself, a carbon copy of his leadership." There was also Titus, a man who could equip and train other leaders. When Paul wrote the epistle to Titus, this leader was at that time leading the church on the island of Crete, which Paul had planted. In that epistle (Titus 1:5, NKJV) Paul writes, "For this reason I left you in Crete, that you should set in order the things that are lacking, and appoint elders in every city as I commanded you."

The appointment of elders in every city was a specific, deliberate process of finding, developing, and empowering leaders across the lands to carry on the vision of spreading the gospel of

Christ. Then there was Luke, Paul's personal attendant. Luke was shipwrecked with Paul and was imprisoned with him. Paul charged Luke with writing histories and accounts of the gospel message, which resulted in two books of the New Testament, Luke and Acts. Mark was a young protégé who had gotten off to a rocky start. Once severely disappointing to Paul, Mark later became "useful for ministry" and was recommended by Paul for leadership. In his letters, Paul mentions other names of those involved in the spread of the early church, and there are perhaps thousands who have gone unnamed.

Both the named and the unnamed became a dynamic legacy to the Level 5 Leadership of the Apostle Paul. He deliberately and painstakingly established followers of leaders across the landscape of the ancient world, establishing a church structure that would train and develop more and more leaders to carry the gospel to the ends of the earth. And that they did. Among the early churches were those in the cities of Troas, Assos, Mitylene, Pergamum, Thyatira, Sardis, Philadelphia, Hierapolis, Smyrna, Magnesia, Miletus, Ephesus, Cos, Cnidus, Rhodes, Myra, Attalla, Perga, Lystra, Iconium, Colossae, Laodicea, Derbe, Seleucia (both in Asia Minor and in present-day Syria), Tarsus (Paul's hometown), Salamis, and Paphos. By the end of the first century, only roughly forty years after Paul's death, this list of churches throughout Asia Minor and Greece and in Rome, Puteoli, and around the Bay of Naples had grown even more.

By the end of the third century, Paul's leaders and their descendants, as well as those of the original apostles, had spread the gospel message of Christ as far north as Britannia (modern-day England) and as far west as the Iberian Peninsula (modern-day Spain and Portugal), and even into northern Africa. Perhaps the most indicative sign of the permeation of Christianity throughout the world is the decision of Roman emperor Constantine in AD 312 to embrace Christianity. By the end of the fourth century,

Christianity would become the official religion of the Roman Empire, the same empire that had executed Paul!

Today, Christianity is the dominant religion in the North American, South American, European, and Australian continents, and is growing most rapidly throughout Russia, China, and many parts of Africa. This is all occurring in places where Paul never traveled and in the lives of people Paul never met, centuries after he lived! That is indicative of the influence of Level 5 Leaders. (*Visions outlive them, grow into movements, and carry on through others over time.*) According to Albert Barnes, "There has been no one of our race who has done so much to determine the theological opinions of mankind as Paul has done." Paul's vision of Christianity spreading throughout the world became so strong, so real, and so enduring that it is impossible to consider Paul without also thinking of his cause. (*The leader grows into his mission.*) As can be said of the causes and visions of true Level 5 Leaders, the world will never be the same.

List a few leaders from your lifetime that you feel have achieved Level 5 Leadership.

_____

_____

_____

What was Paul's legacy?

_____

_____

_____

How has Paul's work continued to impact others?

_____

_____

_____

Why did the work of Paul continue after his death?

_____

_____

_____

What organization, similar to your own, has had a significant leader leave? How did this affect the organization? Why?

_____

_____

_____

Summary

Level 5 Leadership is about making a difference in the status quo that outlives the leader. Level 5 Leaders begin by attracting, inspiring, and enabling leaders who are adept at developing *other* leaders. Only the strongest, humblest, most secure, visionary leaders ever reach this pinnacle of leadership. The results of such ability are astronomical. In *The Effective Executive*, Peter Drucker said, "[No] executive has ever suffered because his subordinates were strong and effective. There is no prouder boast, but also no better prescription, for executive effectiveness than the words Andrew Carnegie, the father of the U.S. steel industry, chose for his own tombstone: 'Here lies a man who knew how to bring into his service men better than he was himself.'"

This chapter and the summary of the life of the Apostle Paul demonstrate that Level 5 Leaders are rare among us. A Level 5 Leader is in a league of his own. He commands the forces of powerful Level 4 Leaders in a productive direction, he's "on fire" for an enormous vision that embraces all of his collective energies, and he leaves a true legacy on the earth. Level 5 is a measure of influence to which every truly inspired, cause-driven, vision-pursuing leader should aspire.

Conclusion

Understanding the Five Levels of Influence

The concept of the Five Levels of Influence is especially helpful for many reasons. First, it helps an individual gauge his own ability and understand how and where to improve. Second, it helps a leader understand where people are in terms of ability and what to do to help them develop. Third, it assists a leader in evaluating the Leadership Level that exists in any portion of his or her *organization*.

The various Levels of Influence also serve to illustrate the concept of the "ability to influence" through the correct actions of a leader. At Level 1, there is no influence, except upon the budding leader himself. At Level 2, the influence can be considered to be "addition," as the efforts of the individual are all that's added to the organization. Level 3 can be thought of as "multiplication" because now the contribution is amplified through a team. Level 4 would then be "exponential" impact because leaders are affecting other leaders, who then lead teams. Level 5 is beyond mathematical description and can only be called a "revolution."

How has learning the Five Levels of Influence helped you the most?

_____

_____

_____

What has been your biggest "Aha!" moment from this workbook?

_____

_____

_____

The Results of Leadership

There is a conversation in the novel *The Sun Also Rises* by Ernest Hemingway in which one character says to another, "How did you go bankrupt?" to which the response is, "Gradually, then suddenly." The compounding effect of leadership is much the same. At first, influence seems very gradual, and even nonexistent, as the leader or the organization enters the learning phase. Then, ever so subtly, performance improves. Out of that performance, leaders arise. From that leadership emerge a few who can lead other leaders. And then, *suddenly*, the results are astronomical.

The point is that leadership is a process. It is ongoing and compounding. It doesn't happen overnight, but over time, it happens in undeniable ways.

Leadership is a _____. It is ongoing and _____.

Walk a Mile; See a Mile Farther

Everybody comes onto the leadership playing field with a different set of innate abilities, but everyone can improve those abilities. The vital component of leadership effectiveness is continual personal growth.

The concept of leadership, which appears so daunting and intimidating to so many people, will become clearer and clearer as the stairs of the Five Levels of Influence are ascended. The leadership journey is not clear when one embarks upon it; but with seasoning, experience, growth in influence, and knowledge, the way becomes clearer. With each new mile traveled, the next mile comes into view. Studying the Five Levels of Influence clears the fog, maps the journey, and allows the aspiring leader to see farther into his own future.

The vital component of leadership effectiveness is continual personal _____.

With each new mile _____, the next mile comes into _____.

Are you able to see yourself as a Level 5 Leader yet? Explain.

_____

_____

_____

What can someone do to better see him- or herself at a higher Leadership Level?

_____

_____

_____

Calling All Leaders

Becoming a leader should not frighten anyone. Rather, it should inspire. Leadership is one of the most rewarding endeavors known to mankind. It is also one of the most important.

Our society is suffering from a leadership crisis. As Edmund Burke noted long ago, "The only way for evil to flourish is for good men to do nothing." There are too many people sitting idly, while the world cries out for leadership. We need leaders in the government, leaders in business, leaders in the community, leaders in the schools, leaders in the homes, and leaders in the churches.

"The only way for _____ to flourish is for good men to do _____."

Why is leadership important today?

_____

_____

_____

Is leadership equally important, less important, or more important today than in the past? Explain.

_____

_____

_____

Ultimately, leadership is a personal responsibility. You have to figure it out as you go, but don't worry: God won't give you a vision without a means to accomplish it.

So come alive.

Get to work.

Lead!